DON'T GO TO LAW SCHOOL (UNLESS)

■ ■ ■

A Law Professor's Inside Guide to Maximizing Opportunity and Minimizing Risk

Paul Campos

Printed in the United States of America

First edition, 2012

ISBN-13: 978-1480163683

ISBN-10: 1480163686

In memory of Warren Myers

Table of Contents

Acknowledgements

This book is a product of conversations with many lawyers, law graduates, law students, and prospective students. Special thanks to Akhil Amar, Deborah Merritt, Kyle McEntee, Deborah Rhode, Fernando Rodriguez, Chris Schilling, Brian Tamanaha, and Elliott Wolf, and to the commenters at *Inside the Law School Scam* and *JD Underground*.

Thanks as well to my agents Jim Levine and Kerry Sparks, at the Levine Greenberg Literary Agency, and to Rebecca Swift for her cover design.

About the Author

Paul Campos is a Professor of Law at the University of Colorado. His previous books include *The Obesity Myth*, *Jurismania*, and *Against the Law* (with Pierre Schlag and Steve Smith). Campos publishes widely in the national media, and his writing has appeared in the *New York Times*, the *Wall Street Journal,* the *Los Angeles Times*, the *New Republic*, and many other publications. He writes a weekly column for Salon.com.

Introduction

THE LAW SCHOOL TRAP

Like a lot of other people, I went to law school because I couldn't think of anything better to do. At the time I applied I was three years removed from my undergraduate days as a somewhat aimless English major, and, while I was enjoying my position as a writer for a small magazine, I was also making the equivalent of $29,000 per year in 2012 dollars. In addition there were rumors the magazine wasn't on stable ground, so I was looking for a backup plan (Indeed the publication went out of business two months before I went back to school).

I had done well in college and – again like uncounted numbers of others – I took the LSAT just to see how I would do. The answer turned out to be well enough to get into an excellent school (Michigan) where I would pay a total of $15,000 in tuition over three years. (At the time, Michigan was actually the most expensive state law school in the nation).

I turned out to have a knack for getting high grades on law school exams, and I got a job with what today would be referred to as a "V10" law firm, where in my first year I was paid a salary five times higher than all of my law school tuition payments combined.

Soon after, I joined the faculty of the University of Colorado, where I've spent the last two decades. Being a law professor is, or at least has been, a ridiculously good job – one which features a much higher salary than most attorneys make today, along with an almost absurd amount of freedom to do almost exactly whatever work you want to do it, when you want to it (or for that matter if you want to do it).

The problem is that, for several years now, I've become increasingly aware that my ridiculously good job is being paid for by people who are increasingly unable to get the kinds of jobs they came to law school to get. A crisis has been building, slowly but surely, in both American legal education and the legal profession as a whole since at least the early 1990s.

For a long time, law schools were able to hide the extent of that crisis, even from themselves, by publishing deeply misleading employment and salary statistics, which for example featured an employment rate that didn't distinguish between a graduate with a job at a top law firm and one working part-time at a coffee shop. These statistics also reported "average" salary numbers that failed to disclose what percentage – often a very small and unrepresentative percentage – of graduates those salary averages represented.

Over the past few years, pressure from lawyers, law students, journalists, politicians, and even a few law professors has forced law schools to begin to disclose more accurate employment and salary data for recent graduates, while better information has begun to be collected regarding educational debt loads, as well as the overall employment picture for lawyers at all levels of the profession.

I have played a role in this movement – I've written several articles for national publications on the subject, and my blog *Inside the Law School Scam* was visited nearly two million times in the first year of its existence – but even I have been repeatedly shocked at just how devastating the real numbers are.

*Only about half of current law school graduates are acquiring jobs as lawyers, even if we define what counts as working as a lawyer in the most generous possible terms.

*The median salary for the national law school Class of 2011 nine months after graduation was around $45,000.

*Some law schools, including some very highly ranked institutions, are putting 20% or more of their graduates into short-term low-paying school-funded "jobs," to boost the schools' reported graduate employment rates.

*Despite such shenanigans, one in every seven 2011 law school graduates was completely unemployed nine months after graduation.

*The average educational debt of new law school graduates is close to $150,000, and rising rapidly.

Here's what these statistics mean in practical terms. An optimistic estimate of the percentage of current law students who will be graduating with degrees that have what economists call "positive net present value" (this means that the cost of their law degrees will be less than the future increased earning potential those degrees will gain them) is around 30%. A more realistic estimate would put the number at about 20%. In other words, it's likely that somewhere around four out of five current law students would be better off if they hadn't gone to law school.

This book is about how to avoid becoming one of them. It's a guide to which law schools are now worth going to at what cost, as well as a warning about the potentially devastating consequences of failing to appreciate the extent to which the average law school degree is no longer worth anything like the price graduates end up paying for it.

Keep in mind that educational debt, unlike almost all other debt in America, cannot except under very rare circumstances be discharged in bankruptcy. What this means is that once you've paid for a law degree, there's no way to walk away from it. If you default on a car loan or a mortgage you can lose your car or your house. If you can't pay your credit card bills you may spend several years struggling to get consumer loans. These are far from trivial consequences; still, all these forms of debt allow the debtor to seek the protection of the bankruptcy laws, and to get a fresh start.

Not so with educational debt. Over the last couple of years, I've heard dozens of heart-wrenching stories from law school graduates who have spent years desperately struggling with an ever-growing mountain of debt. Some have even fled the country to escape their loans (This generally requires going somewhere you otherwise would never want to go). The way our laws treat student debt is a national scandal – one that goes far beyond both the law school crisis and the scope of this book. But it's something anyone considering applying to law school who isn't independently wealthy, or supported by extremely generous family members, must always keep in mind.

Student loans are perilously easy to acquire and, as tens of thousands of law school graduates begin to discover every year, extremely difficult to pay off. The interest alone on $150,000 of educational debt (the average figure now being incurred by law school graduates) is nearly one thousand dollars per month – and that interest accrues onto the principal balance every single day, during law school, and afterwards.

A rule of thumb used by many financial advisers is that people should not incur more educational debt than the annual salary they anticipate making in their first job upon graduation. Some financial experts believe this is too restrictive, and that a debt load 50% larger (that is, a debt to salary ratio of 1.5 to 1) than an initial annual salary is acceptable. Almost all agree that any ratio higher than this is dangerous, and ought to be avoided.

For students currently in law school the average educational debt to salary ratio upon graduation is likely to be 3 to 1 or worse. This is recipe for economic disaster, especially considering that, as we shall see, there is a good deal of evidence that compensation levels throughout the legal profession, and not merely among new attorneys, are declining. The purpose of this book is to help people avoid that disaster, by encouraging them to re-consider law school, unless they really are among the pronounced minority of prospective law students who will be able to attend a law school worth attending, at a price worth paying. *Don't Go To Law School (Unless)* will help you figure out if, at a time when law school is a losing game for most people who play it, you are among the people who have a reasonable chance of winning that game.

The book is divided into fifteen concise chapters, which discuss and explain in straightforward terms the most important things anyone considering law school needs to understand. Generally speaking, the book's first half focuses on the many reasons why anyone considering law school today should approach that decision with extreme caution, while the second half of the book features advice on how to win the law school game, for those who ultimately decide to play it. *Don't Go To Law School (Unless)* explores:

*What the current job market for lawyers actually looks like.

*Why legal education is so often a waste of time in both academic and purely practical terms.

*Why so many law students fall victim to what I call Special Snowflake Syndrome, and how to avoid being one of them.

*How the work lawyers actually do compares to the work law schools want you to think lawyers do.

*Why the claim that a law degree is "versatile" is a dangerous myth.

*Why baby boomers in general, and older lawyers in particular, are likely to give you bad advice about whether you should go to law school.

*How law school scholarships work, and how to get the most money out of any school you're considering attending.

*The opportunities and dangers presented by both law school and government-funded loan assistance repayment programs.

*How to calculate whether attending any particular law school is likely to be worth the cost.

*How to read employment and salary statistics, and how to get the information you really need from any school you're considering attending.

*How to choose between multiple offers of admission.

*Why you should ignore law school rankings.

*How to figure out whether transferring to a different law school is actually worth it.

*How to know if it's time to quit.

*The disturbing rates of depression, substance abuse, and suicide among both law students and lawyers.

*The special temptation law school poses to talented and ambitious young people who seem to have no good career options in our contemporary economy.

I wrote this book because, after more than two decades as a law professor, I'm convinced that law schools are failing in their obligation to put the interests of their students and graduates first. In recent years, too many institutions of higher learning have behaved more like particularly disreputable used car dealerships, rather than places in which the public can confidently put its trust. Law schools have been among the worst offenders in this regard (Indeed, if the kinds of consumer protection laws which are enforced routinely against ordinary businesses were actually applied to law schools, legal academia would have had to clean up its act long ago).

Unfortunately, when it comes to legal education in America, a Latin phrase from the law of contracts continues to have far too much relevance: *caveat emptor* (let the buyer beware). This book hopes to make the potential buyers of law degrees more wary, better informed, and less likely to end up victims of the law school trap.

1

Too Many Lawyers, Not Enough Jobs

Despite what law schools might have you believe, the only good reason to go to law school is to become a lawyer. This, obviously, requires law graduates to get and keep legal jobs. The problem is that, for decades now, law schools have produced far more aspiring lawyers than there are jobs for attorneys – and this mismatch between supply and demand is getting worse all the time.

How bad has it been, and how much worse is it getting? Between 1976 and 2010 ABA-accredited law schools graduated nearly 1.4 million people with J.D. degrees. Unaccredited law schools, located mostly in California where graduates of such schools are eligible to take the bar exam, graduated a couple of hundred thousand more. (I am using this time frame because thirty-five years is a conservative estimate for how long the typical law graduate can be expected to work post-graduation).

So if everyone who graduated from law school over the past thirty-five years were working as a lawyer today, there would be somewhere between 1.4 million and 1.6 million practicing attorneys in America. The actual number, according to the most reliable statistics available – from the federal government's Bureau of Labor Statistics (BLS), which conducts scientific surveys to answer such questions – is 728,000. (The ABA estimates that more than one million people currently hold law licenses, but a large percentage of these people are not practicing law).

In other words, the number of law school graduates produced by American law schools over the past three and half decades is twice as large as the number of practicing lawyers in America today. This number becomes particularly striking if you compare it to the equivalent ratios for doctors and dentists. In those cases, it turns out that, over the past thirty-five years, American medical schools and dental schools have graduated almost exactly as many doctors and dentists as there are doctors and dentists practicing medicine and dentistry in America today.

And with each passing year, the problem gets worse. Consider that, in 2011, ABA law schools graduated 44,458 prospective lawyers. (Unaccredited schools graduated about 8,000 more but I will ignore that complication, although it's one that makes the market for new lawyers worse than it would be otherwise). Meanwhile, the BLS estimates that, between 2011 and 2020, approximately 21,880 jobs for lawyers will become available each year. Two-thirds of these jobs are expected to be from "outflow," i.e., from people leaving the profession, while the BLS predicts the remaining third will be from actual growth in the size of the legal profession.

In other words, if we assume law schools stop expanding, and that every newly available job for a lawyer goes to a new lawyer, as opposed to a formerly unemployed lawyer – needless to say these are both optimistic assumptions – we can project that *less than half* of new ABA law graduates will get jobs as lawyers. But even this understates how dire the job market for new lawyers has become: the BLS projections include temporary and part-time positions – which new law graduates are increasingly forced to take – in that annual total. In addition the projections count a new graduate opening a solo practice – this usually ends up being a more expensive form of unemployment – as the creation of a new legal job. The projections also assume an average annual GDP growth for the economy as a whole of three percent (This is double the rate of average GDP growth over the past decade).

How did we get into a situation where law schools are now producing more than two graduates for every available legal job? The main reason is because for more than 30 years now the market for legal services has been contracting relative to the rest of the economy. Yet law schools, blinded by their own phony employment and salary statistics, continued to expand the size of their graduating classes, while at the same time increasing their tuition many times faster than the rate of inflation.

In 1978 legal services accounted for 2.01% of the nation's gross domestic product. By 2009 that figure had shrunk to 1.37%. In other words, relative to the rest of the economy, the demand for legal services is one third smaller than it was a generation ago. It would be fair to say that until 2011, when a spate of bad publicity in the national media finally forced both the ABA and law schools to begin to acknowledge that law graduates were facing a genuine employment crisis, law schools had paid no attention whatsoever to the fact that fewer and fewer of their graduates were getting jobs as lawyers.

Instead they continued to advertise 95% and 98% and even 100% employment rates for their graduates, without bothering to disclose that many of these jobs included things like part-time low-paid work the graduates could just as easily (actually, as we shall see, more easily) gotten without acquiring a law degree first.

Meanwhile out in the real world, the market for new lawyers was going through a slow motion collapse that started at least as far back as the early 1990s, and only accelerated with the recession of 2007.

And while that recession played a role in the particularly horrible hiring market into which the most recent law school classes graduated, the factors that have produced at least a two to one oversupply of graduates to jobs have little to do with the recession (which has been officially over for three years), and everything to do with structural factors that have changed the practice of law, in ways that have made law degrees much less valuable, even as they have gotten much more expensive to acquire.

These factors include:

(1) Technology. Electronic word search programs now look for specific terms in documents that previously would have been searched for by platoons of highly-paid associates at big law firms. The same legal research that used to take hours before the advent of sophisticated computer data bases now takes minutes instead. As in so many other sectors of the economy, advances in information technology are destroying jobs – in this case legal jobs.

(2) Outsourcing. More and more work that was formerly done by American lawyers is being done by non-lawyers: by paralegals and other legal assistants in the United States, and even by people in other countries (There are tens of millions of Indians who read English perfectly well, and are willing to review documents for far lower rates than the least expensive lawyer in this country could ever charge).

(3) Do it yourself lawyering. While the first two factors affect the amount of legal work billed out by big firms, DIY lawyering is depressing compensation in the world of so-called small law – the little firms or solo practitioners that make a living drawing up wills, corporate documents, divorce papers, and bankruptcy filings for mostly non-wealthy individuals. Online legal document preparation services such as LegalZoom are taking more and more of this work away from lawyers, to the point where small firm attorneys have had to slash their prices for some of their services so much that it's almost impossible for them to make even a modest profit on such work.

(4) Hiring freezes for government lawyers. As of this writing the Department of Justice is into the fourth year of a hiring freeze, and the situation for many cash-strapped state agencies is even worse. Competition for district attorney, public defender, and other government legal jobs has become especially

intense, both because these positions have been disappearing faster than law firm jobs, and because of the financial advantages the new government loan forgiveness programs confer on them (While it takes 25 years to discharge your loans in the government's Income-Based Repayment program, it takes "only" ten in the Public Service Loan Forgiveness program, which applies to government and other non-profit work).

A recent survey by the Alabama Bar Association gives us a glimpse of the effect these changes are having on not just the job prospects for new lawyers, but on the income of experienced attorneys. The survey measures the income levels of lawyers with active licenses in the state in 2009, and compares it to the results of identical surveys done in 1997 and 1985 (the total number of licensed attorneys in Alabama doubled between 1985 and 2009). The results are startling (I've adjusted all dollar figures for inflation):

17% of Alabama attorneys were making at least $200,000 in 1985 in 2009 dollars, while 8.7% of Alabama attorneys were making $200,000 in 2009.

54% of Alabama attorneys were making at least $100,000 per year in 1985 in 2009 dollars, as compared to 28% in 2009.

In 1997 76% of Alabama attorneys were making at least $67,000 per year in 2009 dollars. In 2009 approximately 49% were making at least $67,000.

In 1997, 40% of Alabama attorneys were making at least $134,000 per year in 2009 dollars. In 2009 20% of Alabama attorneys were making at least that much.

Perhaps most significantly, 23% of Alabama attorneys were making *less than $25,000* in 2009, and 37% were making less than $50,000.

These statistics, which mirror the results found by similar surveys in other states, indicate that the percentage of lawyers making a good living practicing law has been cut in half over the last 25 years (Or to put it another way, adjusted for inflation, the total number of lawyers making six figure incomes has remained the same, while the total number of lawyers has doubled). More troubling still, nearly two out of every five lawyers in this survey were earning less than the national median household income ($50,000). This is all the more remarkable given that the average lawyer in the survey had been practicing law for between fifteen and twenty years. (Do not, by the way, believe law school propaganda about how large numbers of baby boomer lawyers are going to retire in the next few years, thus creating lots of new job openings. When calculating future employment opportunities government projections already take historical retirement rates into account, and if anything lawyers are as a matter of economic necessity waiting longer than ever to retire).

At least most of the lawyers in this survey went to law school when getting a law degree was, relative to today, comparatively cheap. Today, law schools apparently expect people to spend $200,000 or more to get a degree which has left increasingly large percentages of experienced attorneys making salaries that are shockingly low, given the investments in time and money they made to enter and stay within the legal profession. Consider that the median salary of new law school graduates is around $45,000, and that law students are now graduating with an average of $150,000 in educational debt, which carries an average interest rate of more than 7%. Even on an extended 25-year repayment schedule, this means the typical graduate in the law school class of 2012 is obligated to pay around 40% of his or her monthly after-tax income toward educational debt, leaving a total of roughly $1,700 per month for all living expenses, including whatever other debt –credit cards, car loans etc. – the graduate may have.

And there's every reason to believe that the structural factors driving down attorney compensation will continue to do so. A lawyer is a knowledge worker whose work represents what economists call a "transaction cost." In a globalized economy, in which technology is constantly reducing the labor costs associated with gathering and interpreting information, American lawyers in particular are seeing the comparative economic advantage that their law degrees gave them continue to deteriorate. (For several years now law schools have been pushing the line that, by the time prospective law students get law degrees, the "present economic downturn" will have ended, and prospects for new lawyers will be better. This is nothing more than a hopeful guess; indeed, given ongoing structural changes in the legal profession, job prospects for attorneys in the foreseeable future are at least as likely to get worse, rather than better).

What All This Means For You

Don't listen to law schools when they claim that, in an increasingly complex information age, the demand for law school graduates is sure to increase. To the extent people who make this argument are not arguing purely out of self-interest, they're confusing *the demand for legal services* with *the demand for the services provided by the graduates of ABA law schools*. In other words, even assuming that going forward the demand for legal services grows relative to the rest of the economy (recall that it has shrunk by a third since the 1970s) that does not mean this demand will be reflected in the future value of law degrees from American law schools.

People who argue that it will can be analogized to someone who would have argued in 1975 that the increasing global demand for automobiles meant that unionized autoworkers had nothing to worry about in the decades to come, because there was sure to be an increase in high-paying union jobs for autoworkers. The effects of technology and outsourcing, which devastated much of the American working class in the 1970s and 1980s, are now having similar effects on the American professional classes. Lawyers have been among the hardest hit by these changes. Make sure that, if you decide to enter a shrinking profession, you do so at a reasonable price, and with your eyes wide open.

2

HOW LAW SCHOOL FAILS

Law school has become a losing game for most people, because the cost of attendance no longer bears any reasonable relationship to the value (if any) that a typical law degree adds to a typical graduate's earning potential. In response to this criticism, especially clueless professors or administrators will sometimes try to argue for the "inherent value" of a legal education, quite apart from the question of whether a law degree is a good investment in terms of dollars and cents.

Leaving aside the obvious absurdity of expecting someone to spend hundreds of thousands of dollars in direct and opportunity costs to acquire something that has "inherent" – as opposed to quantifiable – value, this argument has even bigger flaw: Most of the time, law school is not merely a bad economic investment – it is also a waste of time in both intellectual and practical terms.

This chapter is about how law school fails law students, in ways that go beyond the fact that, for many of them, going to law school ends up being an economic catastrophe. Law school fails because law school faculties are dominated by people who aren't really qualified to provide students with either an intellectually valuable or a professionally useful experience. Law school fails because those people – whether because of tradition, group inertia, or sheer laziness – use teaching and evaluation methods that people who study teaching and evaluation methods agree are highly ineffective, and often strongly counter-productive. Law school fails because law school pretends to be something it isn't, and because those who profit from the status quo have every reason to keep pretending.

Law schools are full of lawyer-academics who are neither lawyers nor academics. Consider the typical career path of people who join tenure-track faculties: after graduating with high grades from a fancy law school, they clerk for a federal judge, then work as junior associates for big law firms for two or three years (sometimes even less), doing the sort of low-level glorified clerical work that junior associates at big law firms generally do. These people then become "law professors."

In other words, these people have no formal training in how to do academic work beyond what they received in law school (which was none), nor do they know more about being lawyer than what they learned in law school, and in very short stints as big firm associates (which was next to nothing). The result is a truly preposterous situation. Other – or perhaps more accurately, real – university departments consider law schools something of a joke: law professors aren't part of a genuine academic discipline, they've never learned to do actual scholarship, and they maintain a ludicrous publication system, which dispenses with peer review in favor of having law students decide what work will appear in the field's "scholarly" journals.

If all this were not bad enough, practicing lawyers tend to be if anything even more contemptuous of law professors than other academics are. Law students have no real sense of how little their professors know about practicing law, but people who have, especially those who have done something beyond being very junior cogs in a giant law firm machine, are well aware of how much sheer fakery goes on in the typical law school classroom.

It's not merely that it's common for a law professor to have never tried a case, or negotiated a deal, or drafted a real-life version of the sorts of documents he's discussing in a Contracts, or Corporations, or Wills and Trusts class – it's that legal academics almost never know anything about the *business* side of legal practice. The two most important practical skills that any lawyer working in private practice must possess are the ability to acquire clients, and to get them to pay their bills, which happen to be two things that most legal academics have never done in their lives.

So people who have never been trained to teach or to do academic research, and who know almost nothing about the practice of law, are expected to teach other people how to practice law, and to spend approximately half their time doing academic research. This by itself is a prescription for disaster, but the situation is made considerably worse by the traditional methods of classroom instruction and evaluation used in law school – methods that most legal academics continue to employ.

The so-called "Socratic method," which involves a professor cold-calling a randomly chosen student and quizzing the student about the facts of an appellate court case, is an absurdly inefficient way to teach people about law. It fills the first-year classroom with significant amounts of fear and anxiety, which anyone who knows anything about educational theory will tell you are exactly the things you want people not to experience when they're trying to learn something. And it fills upper level classes with boredom and detachment, as everyone but the student on the spot zones out and surfs the internet on their laptops.

Of course not all professors use the Socratic method: some lecture, or mix lecture and general discussion with traditional Socratic cold-calling. But the institutional pressure to stick to traditional methods, especially in the crucial first year classes, is often intense. Professors who avoid the traditional methods are often considered less "rigorous," and so many continue to employ these techniques year after year, even if they've come to suspect that they don't actually work very well.

Besides, the great virtue, from the professor's perspective, of the Socratic method is that it's so easy: it takes up large stretches of class time without requiring the instructor to have anything original or interesting to say. (I have witnessed many law school classes, both as a student and a faculty evaluator, in which huge stretches of time were taken up merely reviewing the facts of cases. As one student put it to me, it's as if a good way to study *Macbeth* would be to spend a lot of time asking students where the play took place and who the king of Scotland was).

Even law professors who mostly lecture often have little to say, beyond elaborating the ins and outs of the legal rules touched on in the assigned materials – something that any halfway competent student can learn from the materials themselves, or even more efficiently from the many available commercial outlines that break down law school material much more straightforwardly and coherently than the typical legal academic game of hide the ball, conducted in an increasingly soporific classroom.

A further source of educational dysfunction is that the evaluation method most commonly used in law school – a single end of the semester in-class "issue-spotting" exam – is perhaps the single most absurd aspect of this extravagantly absurd process. Issue-spotting exams, which require students to engage in the pseudo-intellectual equivalent of a game of Where's Waldo, while frantically regurgitating gobbets of legal doctrine they've had stuffed down their throats over the course of the semester, bear no resemblance to anything a lawyer or an academic would ever be expected to do. And they leave students feeling as if their abilities are being evaluated arbitrarily, for the very good reason that they *are* being evaluated arbitrarily (The only thing issue-spotting exams really measure is the ability to take issue-spotting exams. And they do a fairly poor job of even that, as many students discover there's almost no correlation between how hard they study in various classes and the grades they get in them).

Indeed, issue spotting exams persist in law school for the same two reasons so many nonsensical artifacts of legal education are still with us: because they create a relatively small amount of work for law professors, and because law professors did exceptionally well on such exams, so it goes without saying that they must be highly reliable measures of some important skill or ability.

All of these factors combine to produce a level of instruction in law school classrooms that is, on average, quite low. Students who come to law school from good undergraduate colleges are often shocked to discover how badly the typical law school class is taught. I recently got an email from someone who just graduated from a "top tier" law school, after having attended a well-regarded liberal arts college. My correspondent wrote that she had consulted her college and law school transcripts in order to compare the experiences: she concluded that thirty-three of her thirty-five undergraduate courses provided better educational experiences than twenty-six of her twenty-seven law school classes.

This may be a fairly extreme reaction – law schools do employ plenty of bright people, some of whom have a natural talent for teaching – but the fact remains that far too often the law school classroom experience is both intellectually vacuous, and lacks any practical value in regard to learning anything about being a lawyer.

These flaws are exacerbated by the narrow focus of most law school classes, which remain obsessed with analyzing appellate court cases. A depressing number of law school classes consist of nothing more than unnecessarily complicated reviews of various legal doctrines, with a bit of almost always superficial "policy analysis" tacked on. This "case method" of instruction has a certain limited value, but by the second year – to be frank by the second semester – of law school, any halfway able student has learned how to read and argue about appellate court opinions (this is what law schools call "thinking like a lawyer"), meaning that much of the student's second and third years will be wasted in the repetition of an exercise the student masters early on. And this doesn't even touch on the fact that very few lawyers have jobs that require spending much time reading or arguing about appellate court opinions.

And, while all this pseudo-intellectual exercise in doctrinal distinction-drawing and farcically thin "policy analysis" is going on, what are students learning about the actual practice of law? Given that almost none of their teachers know almost anything about the practice of law, the answer, naturally, is "not very much." Some students learn something about legal practice in the law school's legal aid clinics; others learn something while working – often for no pay – for various legal organizations during law school; and members of both groups end up wondering why the classroom component of law school needs to be more than a year long.

Indeed many students end up wondering why law school should be a post-graduate program at all. Couldn't they have learned to read appellate court cases as undergraduates, while being taught by real academics, and then spent a couple of years after college apprenticing with actual lawyers, while learning the basics of practicing law? These are good questions, to which the American legal system provides no good answers. Instead tradition – and more specifically the accreditation standards of the ABA – dictate that students spend three years and a couple of hundred thousand dollars being bored to death by people who are neither academics nor lawyers, but who have managed to convince themselves that they are both.

What All This Means For You

For many law students today, law school ends up being an economic tragedy and an intellectual farce. The tragedy is that every year, tens of thousands of bright, talented young people, full of energy, ambition and hope, discover that their legal educations have left them saddled with life-altering debts, and no realistic way of paying them off. The farce – perhaps it too is a kind of tragedy – is that law school was for these students not merely a bad investment in straightforward economic terms, but something approaching a complete waste of time in terms of either learning things worth learning for their own sake, or mastering some aspect of the vocation to which they felt themselves called.

3

SPECIAL SNOWFLAKE SYNDROME AND HOW TO AVOID IT

Here's a question from a prospective law student, posted on the popular internet message board Top Law Schools in May of 2012:

> So I've been accepted to Hofstra Law as well as California Western. California Western is going to give me a $45,000 scholarship for the three years that I attend. I have two questions:
>
> 1st- Would I be better off moving from California to New York to attend Hofstra (tier 2 school) or stay in California to attend Cal Western (tier 4 school). Basically is it a smart idea to move for a tier 2 school?
>
> 2nd- If I do attend Hofstra can I ever make my way back to California? I hear that wherever you go to laws school most people usually stay in the area because of the networking and job prospects are usually better. I'm just wondering if I stay and work a couple of years and gain some experience in New York will I be able to use that to gain a job in California.

These are both terrible options, as either would involve attending a very expensive law school, which features dreadful employment statistics, and with little or nothing in the way of scholarship money to defray the cost of attendance (The $15,000 per year grant from Cal Western would still leave this prospective student with $180,000 in debt at graduation, assuming the student maintained high enough grades to keep it. Debt financing a Hofstra law degree would result in around $250,000 in debt). Enrolling in either of these schools at these prices is the economic equivalent of mailing yourself a letter bomb.

Nevertheless I hear from prospective law students, or their parents, all the time, asking similar questions to those posed by this hopeful applicant. It's often difficult to tell where on a rhetorical spectrum running from gently tactful to brutally blunt it would be best to put my response. You might think that simply pointing out to people that these schools are extremely expensive and produce, on average, awful results, would be enough to dissuade anyone from going into a couple of hundred of thousand dollars of high interest debt that can't be discharged in bankruptcy to acquire what has an excellent chance of being a worse than worthless degree.

You might think that, but you would be wrong.

Here's why: time and again, when I try to suggest, whether tactfully or bluntly, that spending, or worse yet, borrowing $150,000 or $200,000 or $250,000 to attend a non-elite law school is the very definition of fiscal insanity, I run into a full-blown case of Special Snowflake Syndrome, and end up getting nowhere.

In the world of law school applicants, people suffering from Special Snowflake Syndrome tend to respond to arguments that going to most law schools these days at anything like full price is a terrible idea with one or more of the following claims:

(1) I plan to work exceptionally hard and finish in the top 10% of my class.
(2) After excelling in my first year I will transfer to a much better school.
(3) I have met several very successful lawyers who graduated from the school I'm considering.

(4) If I'm only making $60,000 a year in my first legal job I can go into this government debt forgiveness program that I've heard about – and after all $60,000 is just a starting salary.

(5) There are a bunch of special circumstances about me that make my situation different from those of most people who have my entrance stats.

In other words, statistical extrapolation doesn't really apply in my case, because I am not a statistic. (Interestingly, this belief turns out to be perfectly compatible with a strong belief in the predictive value of statistics when they're applied to other law students).

Let's examine what's wrong with each of these responses:

(1) Almost everyone who goes to law school plans to work exceptionally hard and finish in the top 10% of the class. 90% of these people are going to see their plan fail. (In addition to this hard statistical truth, the arbitrary nature of law school grading practices ensures how hard you work has only a loose relationship to what grades you get. See Chapter 2).

(2) Only the very top of the class at a low-ranked school will have the option of transferring to a high-ranked school. So planning to transfer is just a more extreme version of rationalization number (1).

(3) Rationalization (3) simply consists of paying attention to random anecdotes that confirm what the person wants to believe, and ignoring systematic data which do not.

(4) There are so many things wrong with (4) that discussing them fully requires a separate chapter, and I will address them there. Short version: a $60,000 per year starting salary would be a vastly better than average outcome for graduates of these schools. Many lawyers today find themselves making less money ten years into their careers than they did in their first jobs out of law school. Going into 25 years of debt servitude to the US government both creates a host of new problems of its own, and carries all sorts of risks.

(5) The fifth rationalization is a kind of meta-explanation for why someone believes certain statistical generalizations aren't valid as applied to him, although they are valid when applied to other people who, to all external appearances, look exactly like him. In other words, the applicant believes he is a special snowflake. Statistically speaking, the odds are this belief will turn out to be wrong.

These sorts of rationalizations are very common among people considering going to law school – and indeed if they weren't a large percentage of America's 200 ABA-accredited law schools wouldn't be in business. The reason they're so common can be traced to a pair of cognitive biases that are themselves widespread among people in general and Americans in particular.

Optimism Bias

Most Americans, and particularly upper middle class Americans (i.e., the people who are most likely to go to law school), are socialized to be optimistic. That is, they are encouraged to believe that the chances of a good outcome for them personally are higher than average, and, even more so, that the chances of a bad outcome are lower than average. Of course this is a nonsensical belief from a statistical standpoint, but perhaps the most important element of Special Snowflake Syndrome is that Americans are socialized not to believe in the predictive value of statistics *as applied to themselves as individuals*.

On one level, to believe in the American Dream is to believe that hard work, individual initiative, and belief in yourself can and will overcome whatever obstacles the statistics say are likely to keep you from achieving your goals. One could almost say that the claim that your destiny can be predicted more accurately by statistical generalizations than by the intensity of your belief in your own ability to overcome those generalizations is fundamentally un-American. We are each, supposedly, the masters of our destiny and the captains of our souls, no matter what the Bureau of Labor Statistics might have to say about the matter.

Confirmation bias

People have a strong cognitive bias toward paying attention to information they find pleasing, while ignoring data they find disturbing. This again is a manifestation of how difficult it is for us to genuinely embrace statistical modes of reasoning, at least in regard to ourselves, and subjects we care deeply about. Anecdotes that confirm our biases are interpreted as presumptively meaningful; carefully controlled studies challenging those biases are dismissed as flawed, cherry-picked, and examples of how one can make statistics say anything. As the poet says, "a man hears what he wants to hear and disregards the rest."

Your mission as a prospective law student, should you choose to accept it, is to resist these modes of thinking as much as you can. You can do this by reminding yourself that the most typical outcome for a typical admitted student at a typical law school is . . . the typical one. More specifically, I suggest you engage in two exercises when considering a law school. First, look at the median outcome for graduates. What happens to people who graduate with grades near the middle of the class? (At California Western and Hofstra, the answer is "they don't get jobs as lawyers.").

Second, use what I call the 80% rule. The 80% rule involves ignoring the top ten percent and the bottom ten percent of the class, and then asking what the range of possibilities are if you attend the school in question. The advantage of this approach is that it eliminates outliers, and allows you to determine if an outcome is actually within the likely range of possibilities. For example if, as is the case at the large majority of law schools today, no more than ten percent of the class is acquiring a job with a six-figure starting salary, you should dismiss the possibility of getting such a job as a reason for attending such a school.

On the other hand, if more than ten percent of the class is unemployed or seriously underemployed – that is, doing temporary and/or part-time and/or non-legal work – then you should seriously consider the possibility of such an outcome when considering that school (Unfortunately this means you'll have to consider that possibility if you're considering almost any law school).

It's understandable that prospective law students are even more prone to optimism and confirmation bias than the average American, or even the average college graduate. After all, law students as a group are not average: even at most non-elite schools they have far stronger academic credentials than typical college graduates. Law students are drawn almost exclusively from the top ten percent of the population in terms of basic academic ability, and most come from the top five percent. These are people who have always finished at or near the top of the class everywhere they've been, so it's only natural that they have a deep psychological bias toward assuming they will continue to do so, no matter how conscious the rational part of their minds may be of the fact that only ten percent of a law school's class can finish in the top ten percent.

In this sense first year law school classes in particular are like Lake Woebegone, where all the children are above average. (The most difficult day in the law school calendar is that on which the first year students receive their grades, and discover this isn't true).

Average students at average law schools are by every conventional measure among the best and the brightest of our youth. The sad and dangerous truth, however, is that what has become the absurd cost of law school has combined with long-term structural changes in the employment market to ensure that the average student at the average law school is paying vastly more for his or her law degree than what it's worth.

What All This Means For You

In the context of contemporary legal education, Special Snowflake Syndrome is hazardous to both your emotional and financial health. Sometimes the most difficult thing for talented, ambitious people to recognize is that they are surrounded by lots of other people just like them – and that, despite all their talent and ambition, they are collectively headed for what will turn out to be something between a bad and a catastrophic result.

This, unfortunately, describes the situation at most law schools today. Paradoxically, you can lessen the perils of thinking that you will be an exception to the statistical rules by being the sort of exceptional person that recognizes that you are not, in fact, likely to be an exception to those rules.

4

THERE IS NO SUCH THING AS INTERNATIONAL ENVIRONMENTAL SPORTS LAW

Many people apply to law school while having no real idea what the vast majority of lawyers do. What the vast majority of lawyers do is spend most of their time dealing with mundane business and personal matters. Lawyers do things such as:

(1) Negotiate the legal aspects of business agreements.
(2) Write threatening-sounding letters when disputes arise about such agreements.
(3) Help navigate people through the legal system when they get arrested or divorced, or go bankrupt.
(4) Draft documents to facilitate these and similar transactions.
(5) Sit in courtrooms for hours waiting to appear before a judge for three minutes in order to schedule this or waive that.
(6) Spend time on the phone talking to clients about topics such as why the client is being billed for this phone conversation the client initiated.

Here are some things that very few lawyers ever do:

(1) Argue questions of constitutional law before the United States Supreme Court.

(2) Represent famous athletes or entertainers and hang out at their pool parties.

(3) Prosecute war criminals before the International Court of Justice.

(4) Help the Sierra Club fight a developer's plan to pave over Lake Tahoe.

(5) Vindicate the legal rights of poor people.

(6) Use the legal system to fight social injustice.

Because many of them have no good sense of what being a lawyer usually entails, prospective law students often apply to law school while harboring highly unrealistic career goals. They want to practice "international law" or "entertainment law" or "human rights law" or "environmental law" or "sports law" or even "space law."

It's not as if these practice areas don't exist: indeed, law schools increasingly cater to prospective students by offering specialized programs in these subjects, and *U.S. News & World Report* even provides a series of rankings to supplement their general law school rankings, which purport to inform students which schools have the top programs in ten esoteric specialties. These specialty rankings are ludicrously and laughably useless. For example they suggest to prospective students that it might be better to attend American University – which placed a total of 36% of its 2011 graduates in full-time long-term legal jobs of any kind – than Berkeley or Michigan, if they want to practice "international law." You should not pay the slightest attention to this nonsense.

The site J.D. Underground – an internet gathering place for disaffected lawyers, law graduates, and former lawyers – recently held a mordantly amusing contest to choose the single most preposterous specialty program offered by a law school. The winner of the heated competition ended up being St. John's University School of Law's program in International and Comparative Sports Law, which, as the person who nominated it pointed out, got bonus points for combining international law with sports law, throwing in a very expensive trip to

Madrid, and implying that Big East college basketball tickets might be part of the package.

Here's a quick review of why it's a bad idea to attend law school because you want to specialize in what sounds like an especially fun or politically meaningful area of legal practice. Fields such as international law and environmental law exist, but they: (a) bear very little resemblance to what prospective law students think they involve, and/or (b) they feature jobs that are almost impossible for an entry-level lawyer to get.

Consider "international law." International private law consists mostly of international business transactions, which is a form of large firm transactional work that is indistinguishable from other large firm transactional work, which is to say it features horrendous hours, and requires constant attention to an essentially bottomless well of mind-numbingly detailed documents. If proofreading complex financial statements while having no social life sounds exciting, you'll love "international law" – assuming of course that you get good grades at an elite law school, and can subsequently latch onto a job at one of the relative handful of law firms that do this kind of work.

Of course when prospective students think of international law they're more likely to be thinking – to the extent they're thinking of anything concrete – of international public law, i.e., prosecuting genocidal war criminals before international tribunals, drafting treaties at the United Nations, and so forth. The number of lawyers who do this kind of work is extremely small, and your chances of having a career in international public law can be safely calculated as zero.

A comparable dynamic is at play in environmental law. The most realistic route into the practice of environmental law for an entry-level attorney is to work for a big law firm, which defends corporations against attempts by federal and state governments to sanction them for violating pollution statutes. Not exactly what you had in mind? You could always get a job with a public interest law firm that specializes in defending the environment. Approximately seven people who graduated from law school in 2011 got those kinds of jobs, and all of them finished near the top of their classes at Yale, Stanford, and Harvard respectively, which I suppose could constitute a prospective career plan for the ambitious environmental warrior.

Similar stories could be told about "entertainment law," "sports law," and whatever new sexy-sounding practice area law schools come up with next to extract tuition dollars out of people who aren't willing to face up to the fact that the practice of law almost always consists of some combination of bureaucratic maze-running and small business development. (If law schools wanted to have a specialty program that might actually be of use to their students they could offer certificates in Client Development and Bill Collection. Of course this would require actually hiring onto the faculty someone who knew something about the business side of practicing law).

A word to those who are attracted to law school not because they want to fly to Paris to negotiate Kobe Bryant's next sneaker deal, but because they want to advance the cause of social justice, by for example representing poor and powerless people who are being exploited and oppressed by the rich and powerful. One of the most cynical things law schools do is to play upon the best impulses of idealistic young people, by encouraging people to go to law school not to make money, but rather so they can learn to employ the legal system as a tool for creating a more just society.

In October of 2011, on the White House's official web site, dozens of law schools posted fulsome descriptions of their wholehearted dedication to this goal, after they were asked by the DOJ's Access to Justice Initiative to discuss how they were institutionalizing their commitment to pro bono work and public service. The schools described at length how they encourage their students to represent "under-served" communities, to engage in pro bono (meaning unpaid) work as lawyers, and to pursue careers in public service.

This all sounds quite noble, but needless to say there was no mention, among the thousands of words law schools dedicated to singing their own praises, of certain awkward facts. These include:

(1) The extent to which law schools have chosen over the last three decades to adopt a business model that makes attending law school for any reason other than trying to make as much money as possible simply not practical for most of their graduates.

(2) The refusal of law schools to acknowledge that even those of their graduates who could afford to take low-paying public service jobs are finding it increasingly difficult to get such jobs, in part because law schools have chosen to graduate twice as many lawyers each year as there are legal jobs of any kind.

(3) The fact that law schools have played a key role in creating and perpetuating a legal system which at the same time features a massive oversupply of lawyers, and a scandalous lack of access to legal services.

All of which is to say that, while the desire to go to law school to, as they say, "make a difference" is a commendable one, don't lose sight of the fact that it's becoming harder than ever to use a law degree to work for social change, and that the irresponsible behavior of law schools has contributed to this unfortunate state of affairs. Keep this in mind as you peruse law school catalogs advertising programs in social justice, or poverty law, or whatever else is being taught by limousine liberals with a conveniently poor grasp of the economic relations that pay their six-figure salaries. For it's precisely those relations which are likely to keep you from helping the poor with your law degree (Indeed they are more likely to transform you into a poor person yourself.).

What All This Means For You

It has become difficult enough for law graduates to get any legal job, let alone one in the exotic-sounding specialties that law schools imply will be available to them if they participate in Vermont's "top-rated" environmental law program, or the University of Nebraska's program in Space, Cyber, and Telecommunications Law, or Southwestern Law School's Entertainment and Media Law Institute.

If you go to law school, be sure it's with the goal of doing something more than a tiny handful of lawyers actually do. And remember that, if you want to work for social justice, you don't need a law degree – and indeed at present getting a law degree is more likely to impede your pursuit of that goal than advance it.

THE MYTH OF THE VERSATILE
LAW DEGREE

Now that somewhat reliable statistics regarding employment and salary outcomes for recent law graduates are finally becoming available, law schools are facing a serious problem: It's increasingly clear that there are far too many law school graduates chasing far too few legal jobs, and that the number of jobs for lawyers that pay enough to justify the cost of law school is much smaller still (See Chapter 1).

Law schools could respond to this crisis by undertaking real reform, by for example producing far fewer graduates while charging a much lower price of attendance. Such reforms would require very painful changes within legal academia (many law schools would have to close, while others would need to make their faculties work much harder for quite a bit less money), so instead law schools have to this point largely rejected serious reform in favor of attempts to market their way out of trouble.

Schools build shiny new buildings full of luxurious features – an example of what is known in higher education as the amenities race. They print glossy brochures advertising programs in environmental justice and international human rights and sports and entertainment law (see Chapter 4). They offer generous –sounding "scholarships," which give prospective students the impression they're getting a great deal to attend (see Chapter 7). But perhaps the favorite marketing ploy law schools use when critics point out that huge numbers of their graduates aren't actually getting jobs as lawyers is to claim that a law degree is" versatile."

It's quite true you can do many things if you have a law degree. The problem is you can also do all those things if you don't have a law degree – except practice law. Nevertheless, law school administrators, desperate to pull future tuition dollars out of a shrinking applicant pool, are increasingly resorting to sometimes comically over the top arguments about how "versatile" a law degree supposedly is.

Here is Harold Krent, dean of Chicago-Kent College of Law:

> I think that there's been a significant distortion in terms of the drying up of the legal market in the media. It's actually true at large firms in the last couple of years. But there has not been a commensurate drop off in smaller firm and government practice.
>
> Many people do wonderfully creative and interesting things with a law degree other than practice law, including being a journalist or being an investor or being a counselor.

Krent's assertion that smaller firm and government practice hasn't been hit as hard by changes in the legal market as big firm law is actually the opposite of the truth, but the really outrageous part of the quote is the claim that one can employ a law degree to become a journalist or an investor or a counselor. It should be unnecessary to point out that absolutely nothing about law school prepares one to practice journalism or counseling (As for being an "investor," the only pre-requisite for that occupation is having a lot of money to invest).

Krent, to the extent he's not just making stuff up on the fly, is falling prey to the myth that law school imbues those who undergo it with marvelously transferable analytic skills – the idea, in short, that learning to "think like a lawyer" (whatever that means) somehow prepares one to do all sorts of things that have no relation to actually *being* a lawyer.

An even more amusing – and infuriating – example of this sort of thing is provided by Duquesne Law School dean Ken Gormley, who in a newspaper opinion piece upbraids people who plan to go to law school to make money instead of to "seek justice" (Duquesne's graduates are currently leaving the school with an average of around $120,000 in law school debt alone, which is going to make seeking justice for its own sake an extremely expensive proposition). He then points out that there are a lot of things you can do with a Duquesne law degree besides practice law, such as become president of the Pittsburgh Steelers NFL franchise.

Gormley fails to mention that the Steelers' president is the grandson of the team's founder, which might just possibly have more to do with his acquisition of that job than his Duquesne law degree.

This is just a particularly extreme example of the absurd way law schools credit themselves for the career successes of their graduates who aren't lawyers, even when there isn't the slightest evidence that going to law school had anything to do with that success. And, in an economy where more than half of law school graduates won't have careers as lawyers, there are going to be a lot more "success stories" of people who went to law school, couldn't get jobs as lawyers, and did things like eventually found a string of profitable yoga studios instead (When you're cranking out 25,000 graduates every year who will end up having to do something other than practice law, some of them will inevitably be quite successful doing something completely unrelated to their legal education).

Of course some law school graduates who don't practice law do end up in jobs where their law degrees helped advance their careers. For example, a few law school graduates end up in corporate compliance positions, which help corporations follow legal rules and regulations (These positions are usually not held by people with law degrees, but a law degree is sometimes considered a desirable credential for an applicant to have).

On the other hand, my colleague Deborah Merritt, who studies changes in the market for legal services, points out that corporations have learned it's much cheaper to hire people without law degrees to do a great deal of legally-related work that used to be done by lawyers: "Companies have discovered," she says, "that college-educated workers can read and apply legal regulations without first earning a law degree." Indeed, "with on-the-job training, supportive software, and a few lawyers at the helm, BAs can also interview people and draft legal documents. Those BA workers can even conduct legal research and advise their companies on relevant legal changes."

When tracking employment outcomes for law graduates, the ABA maintains a category of so-called "JD advantage" jobs – positions that don't require a law degree, but which are categorized either by the graduates who obtained them or by the law schools who report the data as jobs where the graduate's JD played a role in obtaining it. (In 2012, 9% of new law graduates were categorized as employed in such jobs nine months after graduation – with how much accuracy it's difficult to say).

But there's a flip side to claims, whether accurate or not, that a JD helped someone get a non-legal job. This is what can be called the "JD disadvantage" category: jobs that people aren't able to get precisely *because* they have a law degree.

There's a great deal of evidence that suggests this category is actually quite a bit larger than the JD advantage category – that, in other words, on balance having a JD does more harm than good to the law school graduate who, by choice or necessity, is trying to get a job outside the legal profession. Rather than being a versatile degree, many graduates discover that a JD can be a toxic asset – one which they end up having to try to purge from their resume in order to move on with their careers once they've given up on entering or staying inside the legal profession.

What can make a law degree something that people end up hiding rather than highlighting? Four factors help transform law degrees into toxic assets for law school graduates who try to obtain work outside the legal profession:

(1) Non-legal employers assume that an applicant with a law degree is just marking time until he or she leaves for one of the many high-paying legal jobs that non-lawyers mistakenly believe most people with law degrees hold (In fact less than a quarter of working age Americans who have law degrees made $75,000 or more practicing law in 2011).

(2) Non-legal employers naturally wonder why someone with a law degree doesn't want to – or worse yet can't – practice law. Again, people outside the legal profession understandably don't have a good sense of how terribly oversaturated the market for attorneys has become, and how difficult it is for lawyers to establish and maintain legal careers. Instead they will tend to see the inability or unwillingness of a law graduate to continue to pursue such a career as a warning signal regarding the person's possible defects, as opposed to a product of structural unemployment within the legal profession that the job candidate can do nothing about.

(3) Non-legal employers don't like the idea of hiring someone who they imagine will have a sophisticated understanding of employment law, and has been supposedly trained to sue people at the slightest provocation.

(4) Non-lawyers don't like lawyers.

Time and again, in the course of studying the collapsing market for both law graduates and experienced lawyers, I have encountered people who tell some variation of the same story: after a year, or two, or longer, of trying unsuccessfully to establish or maintain a legal career, the person started looking seriously for non-legal jobs. Remarkably often, these stories have the same conclusion: not until these people removed their law degree from their resumes were they able to begin to have some success in securing any non-legal job.

Taking your law degree off your resume is not as simple as it sounds: how, for example, are you supposed to explain what, between law school and a failed attempt to establish a legal career, is often a five to seven-year gap in your life story? (Experienced attorneys who leave the profession face an even more difficult task in this regard).

Such people have spoken movingly to me of how hard they tried to make a career for themselves in law, and how shocked they were to discover that, far from giving them an advantage against other job candidates for non-legal positions, their law degrees stigmatized them. Perhaps the starkest stories were told by former paralegals, who left reasonably well-paid, stable positions in the legal profession to go to law school, and then found that, after getting law degrees and failing to establish careers as lawyers, they were unable to return to their former profession (It's commonplace for advertisements for paralegal positions to explicitly refuse to consider applicants with law degrees).

What All This Means For You

Far from being "versatile," a law degree can turn into a toxic asset for law school graduates who, by choice or necessity, look for work outside the legal profession. If you go to law school and end up not practicing law, there's a real risk that you'll find your law degree is actually worse than worthless, and that you would have been better off not getting it even if you could have gotten your degree for free.

This is yet another reason – and perhaps the most important – why the only people who should go to law school are people who genuinely want to be lawyers, who have good reasons for believing this desire is based on some at least minimally realistic knowledge of what being a lawyer involves, and who can do so at a reasonable price.

6

MY SON THE LAWYER IS DROWNING: HOW TO DEAL WITH CLUELESS BABY BOOMERS

There's an old Jewish joke – it appears in Philip Roth's novel *Portnoy's Complaint* – about a woman running down a Florida beach shouting "Help, my son the doctor is drowning!" This joke wouldn't work if the son were an accountant or a businessman, let alone a policeman or a plumber. It would work – although given the ubiquity of lawyer jokes in a somewhat ironic way – if the son were a lawyer. (Note how a businessman who flourishes in his trade is invariably described as "a successful businessman" while by contrast nobody ever refers to "a successful doctor", and only rarely to "successful" lawyers. That's because a doctor, unlike a businessman, is considered a social success simply by virtue of being a doctor).

While there's no question that in America today more social prestige attaches to doctors than to lawyers, doctors and lawyers are the two most commonly cited professions when people speak in an offhand way about social mobility in general, and more specifically about the relationship between educational opportunity and the American dream, so-called (If you type "a doctor or" into Google, the first auto-fill will be "a lawyer.")

There's a good deal of cultural cachet attached to the social identity of the lawyer, or more pompously "the attorney at law." An economist would say there are "psychic benefits" to being a lawyer that go beyond the monetary benefits of a legal career (there are also, as we shall see, psychic costs). The psychic benefits that flow from the social prestige that's attached to being a lawyer are often sought after by the families of prospective law students, who want their children to do something with their lives in which the family can take pride.

As the word about the risks of attending law school starts to get out among prospective students, I've heard from quite a few people who find themselves in some variation of the following dilemma: A law school applicant graduated from college a year ago and has either been working at a low-wage low status job, or has been volunteering for a social service organization. The applicant has been offered partial "scholarships" (cross-subsidized tuition breaks; see Chapter 7) to low-ranked law schools, or could attend a higher-ranked but not elite school at sticker price.

The parents are putting major pressure on applicant to enroll, by offering some financial support, such as promising to cover the applicant's living expenses while in law school, or offering to make the applicant's loan payments for a year or two after graduation.

The applicant has done some research and realizes the available options don't look good, but either doesn't want to alienate the parents and/or wants the offered financial support. The applicant has tried to convince the parents that the wise thing to do under the circumstances is to re-take the LSAT and try to get better offers in the next admissions cycle, but the parents are rejecting this idea.

In all these cases I've been struck by the extent to which some type of status anxiety seems to be driving the parents' actions. Often the applicant is from an upwardly mobile professional class family which came to the US in the previous generation. Another common scenario involves a parent who has had a successful legal career (but apparently will not be in a position to exercise much if anything in the way of nepotistic influence).

These applicants– they tend to be young people who have yet to do much with their lives besides go to school – are getting the message that their parents are frustrated by what they perceive as post-college drift, and are impatient to see their children take on the respectable professional identities that they were sent to school, often at considerable expense, to acquire.

It appears the parents simply don't believe what their children tell them about what has happened to the relative value of a law degree. This is especially a problem for the child of the lawyer who graduated from law school 25 years ago from a state law school, after paying a total of $7,000 over three years in tuition. This parent will often claim to have "struggled" to get a job, which turns out to mean he or she had to work for two years at a legal job the parent didn't really want before getting the kind of job he or she had gone to school to acquire.

In short, the parents of these prospective law students refuse to accept that, in America today, it's perfectly possible for people from relatively privileged upper middle class backgrounds to follow all the rules, do everything right, and still end up with a series of bad career options. It's as if they refuse to believe something like that could be the case. They push their children to make what is likely to turn out to be an irreversibly bad choice in the long run, so that at least in the short run they can say their children are going to be something that still sounds like a good thing to be.

If you find yourself in this sort of position, keep a few things in mind:

(1) The conventional wisdom about education debt in general, and law school debt in particular, being "good" debt has fallen very far behind the new reality of a lost generation of highly educated young people, who are unable to get jobs that come anywhere close to paying enough to service the loans they took out to get these supposedly valuable degrees. Ironically,

parents who don't have any real sense of the extent of this generational crisis – and many don't – are prone to misinterpret their better informed child's hesitancy to embark on an expensive and risky professional career track as immature postgraduate slacking, rather than seeing it as the commendable prudence it actually represents.

(2) Many older lawyers have literally no idea how much it now costs to get a law degree. I run into this continually: people who graduated from law school in the 1970s and 1980s are frankly incredulous when I quote current tuition costs to them. (Thirty years ago, tuition at Harvard Law School was $6,200 per year – the equivalent of $15,000 per year today. And Harvard was one of the most expensive law schools in the country. Many state law schools charged $100 per month in tuition).

(3) Although older lawyers generally aren't as clueless about the contracting legal market as they tend to be about the current cost of law school, many still have only a very limited sense of how that bad that market is getting for both new and experienced attorneys. If you have a relative who maintains a currently successful practice, or is in a stable government job, it's quite possible this person has a very inadequate sense of how bad the job market for lawyers really is (Experienced lawyers who lose their jobs – especially partners at prestigious firms who are let go because they're not bringing in enough business or because the whole firm falls apart – undergo an extremely harsh form of reality therapy in this regard).

In other words, what the prospective law student who is being pressured to make a bad choice in regard to law school is dealing with is a kind of generation gap. On one side of that gap, often clueless baby boomers exhort their children to follow life rules that made sense for their own generation, but no longer do for their children.

On the other are the children themselves, who must deal not only with the anxieties produced by their precarious social and economic situation, but also with the frustration of trying to explain the true nature of that situation to people who on some level don't want to believe that following all the rules they taught their children to follow could have produced the outcome it has produced.

If you must deal with parents or other relatives or family friends who don't understand that paying what most law schools today charge most of their students to attend is for most students somewhere from a bad to an utterly catastrophic decision, don't forget that you're the one who will have to live with the consequences of what needs to be truly your own decision, and no one else's.

This can be especially difficult if your family is offering financial incentives for you to make a decision you would certainly not make if it were your own money. But even if your family should offer to bear the entire direct cost of law school, going to a school you would not go to if you had to borrow the money is still a very problematic choice. Naturally you don't want to waste your family's resources on a bad investment, but you also don't want to end up dealing with the consequences of not having the sort of career your family thought it was paying for.

Of course the typical prospective law student is going to have to borrow most or all of the money he or she will pay to whatever schools the student is considering. In this circumstance, it's especially important not to give in to any pressure from people who, much as you may love them, simply have little or no idea what they're talking about. You can try your best to convey this truth (I would recommend trying to do so in more tactful terms than those I'm employing), by showing them the real statistics on law school debt, legal jobs, and lawyer salaries.

Some will listen, some won't, but in the end it's your life. One thing is certain: if you're not ready to stand up to your family on this matter, you certainly aren't ready to decide to go to law school, let alone to practice law. And there's no shame in that: the assumption that every 22-year-old college senior is ready to decide whether it's really a good idea to incur $200,000 in debt while attempting to become a lawyer is how we got into this mess in the first place.

What All This Means For You

The cost of law school and the likely future return on a law degree have both changed so radically over the past twenty years, and especially over the past decade, that many older people, and even many older lawyers, have no idea how risky a proposition law school has become. Rather than relying on the conventional wisdom, do your own research about costs and likely outcomes. I would especially recommend talking to an assortment of recent graduates of any law school you're considering seriously (Don't ask the school for names: look people up on the bar registry of the state where the school is located.). Talk to people about both their own experiences and those of their classmates. You'll get a much clearer picture from this exercise than from chatting with Name Partner, who graduated from State U during the Carter administration, when tuition was $400 per semester, and when there were nearly as many legal jobs as there were law school graduates.

7

THE REVERSE ROBIN HOOD PRINCIPLE: HOW LAW SCHOOL "SCHOLARSHIPS" WORK

Law schools like to present themselves as pure meritocracies, but the reality is quite different. Law is a particularly status-obsessed profession, so it's not surprising that people who come to law school with both lots of money and what sociologists call "cultural capital" – this means people who already know the rules of how high social status games are played – tend to do much better in the law game than people from less privileged backgrounds.

This chapter is about how law students pay for law school, and in particular how what law schools call "scholarships" actually work. The quotation marks signal that with few exceptions law school grants are not scholarships in the traditional sense – that is, endowed funds that generate income which is used to pay for part or all of the recipient's attendance costs. Rather, law school scholarships almost always consist of cross-subsidized tuition grants.

Here's a simplified example: Suppose Acme Law School charges a nominal tuition of $40,000 per year, but half the students are actually charged less. The half of the class that pays less than the nominal tuition receives an average discount of $12,000 off the nominal price. Thus the average tuition paid by Acme students is $34,000 (half the class pays $40,000, while the other half pays an average of $28,000). In effect, the students who pay $40,000 subsidize the tuition paid by their classmates who pay less.

Let's look at what effects this system has at a couple of elite law schools, particularly in regard to the "average" debt loads carried by graduates of these schools, and the effects different debt levels will have on the long-value various graduates receive from their law degrees (As we shall see, "average" in this context can be a misleading term). Doing so will give us a glimpse of the powerful role socio-economic status plays within elite contemporary American institutions.

Law school has gotten astonishingly expensive: elite law schools charge an average of more than $50,000 per year for three years of tuition. In addition most elite schools are located in very expensive cities, and ABA regulations prohibit students from working more than 20 hours per week during law school (These restrictions are sometimes ignored by students, but this can be risky, as violating these rules could at least in theory lead to a "character and fitness" issue when applying to take the bar).

As a result, the direct cost of law school attendance is now approaching $250,000 at some schools (this figure ignores the opportunity costs incurred by people who take themselves out of the labor market for three years). For most students, this produces a crushing load of high interest educational debt, that isn't dischargeable in bankruptcy. On the other hand, a remarkably large number of students manage to graduate from elite law schools with no debt at all. How does this happen?

The answer isn't that law schools give out big scholarships. In contrast to most graduate programs, full tuition scholarships to law school are rare, and grants of full tuition plus any kind of significant living stipend are even rarer. Indeed with the exception of Yale, Stanford, and Harvard, law schools give out very little need-based air: almost all grants come in the form of "merit scholarships," i.e., payments designed to induce prospective students with high LSAT and GPA numbers to enroll. (Yale, Stanford and Harvard claim that all their aid is need-based). Yet the vast majority of these merit "scholarships" aren't really scholarships at all – they are merely cross-subsidized tuition discounts.

Let's see how this plays out in the context of two elite law schools. Columbia estimates that cost of attendance for the 2012-13 academic year will be $79,950. This includes $59,270 in tuition and fees, and $20,680 for nine months of living expenses (This does not seem like an extravagant budget for Manhattan, plus it doesn't include the fact that students have to pay for three months of additional living expenses).

Last year 51% of CLS students paid sticker tuition. 37% paid more than half sticker tuition, 9.5% paid less than half sticker tuition, 1.6% paid no tuition, and 0.7% paid no tuition and got some sort of stipend (probably enough to cover the cost of books). The median grant for students who got grants was $13,200, so the real average tuition in 2012-13 is going to average around $53,500. When one includes living expenses the real average cost of going to Columbia right now is about $220,000. (This doesn't include summer living expenses). If you borrow this sum in federal loans then you will, because of interest accrued during law school, owe $256,000 when your first loan payment becomes due six months after graduation.

Northwestern has a projected cost of attendance for 2012-13 of $79,628 (again, this doesn't include three summers worth of living expenses). Last year 69.4% of Northwestern students paid sticker, 21.3% paid more than half tuition, 9.3% paid less than half tuition, and no student got a full tuition grant. The median grant for the 30.6% of the class that received one was $20,000, making the projected real average three year-cost of attendance for the 2012 entering class $218,000 (I am very conservatively and unrealistically projecting no tuition increases). If financed through federal loans, this will result in a loan balance of $254,000 six months after graduation.

In short more than 90% of the students attending these two law schools are paying at least $150,000 in direct expenses to do so, and the large majority pays well more than $200,000. And basically no one who attends Columbia or Northwestern spends less than $65,000 to $80,000 over the course of law school, since everyone pays three full years of living expenses.

(It's true that most of the students who attend these elite schools make about $20,000, after taxes, as summer associates after their second year of law school – a sum which more or less offsets three summers worth of living expenses they incur between starting law school and taking the bar).

Now here's the punch line: no less than one out of four of the students who graduate from these schools – 23% of Columbia grads, 27% of Northwestern grads – *finish law school with no law school debt whatsoever.* In other words, something close to one in four grads of these elite schools come from family backgrounds that allow them – or more accurately allow their parents – to pay, in most cases, somewhere between $150,000 and $250,000 *in out of pocket cash* for the cost of law school.

What about the other three quarters of the class? Well, the 2011 classes at Northwestern and Columbia graduated with a putative average law school debt, among those graduates who had such debt, of $140,000 and $133,000 respectively. But these numbers, daunting though they are, are actually quite misleading. First, they are averages not medians. They include quite a few graduates from well off, but not extremely rich, families who for example paid all of the graduate's tuition, but left the graduate to take out loans for some or all of the graduate's living expenses. The median debt for the three quarters of the class with debt is certainly a good deal higher – as indeed it has to be, given that the average real cost of attendance at these schools is over $200,000.

The reported debt numbers are deceptive in another way: *they don't include accrued interest.* What's called "average" law graduate debt in media reports on the subject is significantly under-reported, because law schools don't report graduate debt to the ABA: they report the average amount of federal educational loans disbursed to their students – a significantly lower number. Interest accrues on law school loans as soon as they're disbursed (Formerly the first $8,500 per year of loans did not have interest accrue because they were sub-sidized; this subsidy was eliminated in the summer of 2012).

What this means is that a graduate who took out $140,000 in loans had, when the first of the loan payments became due in November of 2011, approximately $160,000 in actual loan debt. Someone who borrowed $200,000 (a reasonable estimate of the *median* amount borrowed by Columbia and Northwestern students who took out any loans at all) had $232,000 in law school debt by that point (And keep in mind these figures don't include undergraduate or other educa-tional debt).

None of this has touched on the ultimate irony that, in general, the higher a student's socio-economic status (SES), the less that stu-dent tends to pay in tuition. Remember "merit scholarships" – that is, offers of discounted tuition – are used by almost all law schools to buy higher LSAT and GPA numbers, and for what should be obvious rea-sons high SES tends to correlate strongly with high numbers. (High SES bestows enormous relative advantages in regard to access to the sorts of resources that produce both high standardized test scores and college grades). So, on average, law students who come from lower SES backgrounds subsidize the tuition of those who come from privileged backgrounds. (This has been called the "reverse Robin Hood" principle).

But the reverse Robin Hood principle doesn't' end there: in addition to graduating with less debt, the high SES graduates are far more likely to have a nepotistic leg up for high status legal jobs, since quite a few hiring decisions for those sorts of positions end up getting made by somebody whose son graduated from Phillips Andover just a year after the ultimately successful job candidate. Social and economic connections have always been Important to success in the practice of law, and, as American society becomes increasingly stratified, they are if anything likely to become even more so. Those who go to law school without such connections are at a serious disadvantage in relation to their classmates who are more fortunate in this regard. Perversely enough, law students with few or no connections and consequently poorer job prospects, are, on average, subsidizing those with "merit" scholarships – many of whom, to quote a famous quip about a politician from an especially privileged background, are the kind of people who were born on third base but think they hit a triple.

What All This Means For You

If you don't come from a privileged background, even the most elite law schools have become dangerous propositions. Your classmates who do come from such backgrounds will finish with an enormous advantage over you, both in terms of what law school has actually cost them (in many cases, nothing but time), and in terms of what sorts of jobs they are likely to be offered, and can afford to take. And keep in mind that as the competition for legal jobs becomes ever-more fierce, the social and economic elites will use all the considerable power at their disposal to make sure their children get the lion's share of the sorts of positions that people go to elite law schools in order to be able to get.

8

DEBTS NO HONEST MAN CAN PAY: LRAP and IBR

Law students today are incurring educational debt loads that they won't be able to pay back in anything like a timely manner, given the kinds of legal jobs (if any) they're getting when they graduate. Current law students will, conservatively speaking, graduate with an average of about $150,000 in educational debt. This debt will carry an average interest rate of over seven percent, meaning that repaying it over a standard ten-year period will require monthly payments of around $1,775, and repaying it over the "extended" 25-year period still requires monthly payments of $1,100.

Given that the median salary for graduates of the law school class of 2012 is around $45,000 – a sum which equals an after-tax income of around $2,800 per month – this means a huge percentage of current law students will not be able to service their debts according to the contractual terms of their loan agreements.

In a well-functioning credit market, it shouldn't be possible for people to borrow amounts of money that they have no realistic prospect of paying back. But the market for law school loans suffers from an enormous distortion: currently, the federal government will loan any admitted student who isn't already in default on an educational loan the full cost of attendance to attend any ABA law school – *and that cost is determined by the school.* In other words, a law school can charge literally anything it wants to charge for tuition, and the federal government will loan that amount (plus the cost of living while attending) to any admitted student. This is naturally a prescription for the massive overpricing of law degrees, which is exactly what has happened.

This radical disconnect between the debt students are incurring and the return they're getting on their investment is requiring law schools to come up with creative ways to convince students to take on debts they won't be able to repay. To understand what law schools are trying to sell in this regard, it's necessary to understand what traditional Loan Repayment Assistance Programs (LRAP) have looked like.

For decades now, a handful of elite law schools have had programs where all or a substantial part of a graduate's law school debt was paid by the school if the graduate went into public interest law, rather than taking a job with a private law firm. The logic behind these programs was that graduates who took this career path were sacrificing high salaries by using their law degrees to pursue public service rather than private profit, and therefore it was appropriate for the law school to subsidize this choice. (Of course in practice this means that graduates working for private firms were, via their own debt loads, actually subsidizing their classmates' less lucrative career choices).

For the economics of such a program to work, it was necessary for the number of graduates going into high-paid private legal work to vastly outnumber those going into public interest law. Since such ratios existed at only the most elite law schools – which were also the schools which had substantial endowments that could help pay for these programs – the vast majority of law schools either had no LRAP at all, or only token programs. And this is still the situation today – with one very significant change.

As student debt has become a pervasive problem throughout higher education, Congress has created a pair of programs that allow graduates to pay less than the full amount they owe on their educational loans. Income-Based Repayment (IBR) and Public Service Loan Forgiveness (PSLF) work like this: If a graduate's income is below a certain level relative to the graduate's federal educational loan debt, the graduate who enrolls in the program is allowed to make payments for less than the full amount owed – sometimes far less. Consider the case of a law school graduate who has $150,000 in federal educational loans, and is making $45,000 per year. If the graduate is enrolled in IBR or PSLF, the graduate is required to make a monthly loan payment of just $350, rather than the $1,100 the graduate would have to make under the extended 25-year repayment schedule. If the graduate remains in IBR for 25 years, the debt the graduate still owes is forgiven at that point. If the graduate is in the PSLF program – which requires working for a non-profit employer – the graduate's debt is forgiven after ten years.

To superficial appearances, IBR and PSLF look like federally-funded LRAP programs – and indeed as we shall see, almost all of the small number of law schools that have substantial LRAP programs have now bootstrapped their programs to IBR and PSLF. Meanwhile the vast majority of law schools, which either have no LRAP at all, or merely token versions of such programs, are aggressively promoting IBR and PSLF to prospective students, as a reason to take on massive debt to acquire a law degree from these schools.

The truth is that people who are likely to end up in IBR and PSLF if they go to law school should not go at all. While preferable to actually defaulting on one's loans, these programs are fraught with disadvantages and dangers for those who will be forced to employ them. These include:

(1) A graduate who pays less than the full interest owed on the graduate's loan each month sees his or her loan balance grow. For example in the case above, in which the graduate pays just $350 per month on a $150,000 balance, that balance will grow by nearly $10,000 for every year in which the graduate's debt to income ratio remains the same. This growth makes it increasingly unlikely that the graduate will ever be able to pay back, or perhaps even reduce, the balance of the graduate's loan.

(2) The graduate will have an enormous unsecured debt on his or her credit record, which will make it difficult or impossible to secure other forms of credit, especially home mortgages.

(3) Under IBR, while the balance of the loan is forgiven after 25 years, the forgiven amount is treated as taxable income. This means that, in the eyes of the IRS, if the government forgives $300,000 worth of debt, it's as if the person who has the debt forgiven earned an extra $300,000 the year the debt was forgiven, and he or she is presented a tax bill that reflects this.

(4) The program doesn't create any contractual rights, and it could be changed or eliminated at any time. Indeed, the federal budget resolution passed by the House of Representatives in 2012 proposed eliminating IBR altogether. (The resolution's author was Paul Ryan, who later in the year Mitt Romney chose as his vice presidential running mate).

PSLF, which forgives debt after ten years rather than twenty-five, and under which forgiven debt is not treated as taxable income, is, from the perspective of the debt-ridden graduate, much preferable to IBR. But this too creates a downside for prospective law students: public interest jobs, which are already extremely competitive, are becoming even more difficult to acquire, as lawyers in such jobs who carry large debt loads become increasingly unwilling to leave them, so they can take advantage of PSLF's favorable terms.

None of this is stopping law schools from aggressively market-ing IBR and PSLF as "solutions" to the economic crisis created by their granting of tens of thousands of vastly overpriced law degrees every single year. (Given that the American taxpayer will be left hold-ing the bag for all the unpaid debt accrued by law graduates in these programs, there's a good argument to be made that law schools who promote IBR are participating in a fraud on the public. Consider too that to be eligible for these programs you must be enduring what the programs define as significant "financial hardship." Do law schools really want to promote the idea that getting a law degree is likely to make many of their graduates eligible for what are in effect federal welfare programs?).

Even elite law schools – the only ones that have ever had real LRAP programs – are jumping onto the IBR gravy train, by integrating their programs with it. They are doing so by requiring their graduates who want to take advantage of the schools' LRAP programs to enroll in IBR first. These schools then limit their LRAP contribution to paying the graduates' IBR payments. For example, the graduate with $150,000 of debt and the $45,000 job would, if he or she graduated from one of these elite schools, get a $350 monthly benefit from the school's LRAP program, but would still see his or her loan balance climb every month. In other words, IBR is allowing these elite schools to greatly scale back on their previous commitment to actually paying the law school debts of those of their graduates who go into public service.

What All This Means For You

When law schools push the supposed benefits of IBR and PSLF to prospective students, what they're really doing is advertising that they're operating under a business model that doesn't work unless it's subsidized heavily at both ends by the American taxpayer. Law school is subsidized on the front end by federal educational loans, which allow students to borrow money they won't be able to pay back, and by IBR and PSLF on the back end, which allow graduates to have the "privilege" of being in debt servitude to the U.S. government for ten or, more likely, twenty-five years, with the added bonus of being hit by a huge tax bill at the end of it all.

Here's a question law schools keep hoping doesn't get asked: if there's a massive oversupply of lawyers in America, to the point where half of all new law graduates aren't getting legal jobs at all, why is the federal government issuing billions of dollars of taxpayer subsidies every year to produce twice as many new lawyers as the economy can absorb, at a vastly higher price than they would be produced if those subsidies didn't exist?

If you go to law school, make sure you do everything you can to avoid being stuck in IBR when the political process starts addressing that question. You can be sure law schools aren't going to like the answer.

9

TIME AND MONEY: WHEN IS LAW SCHOOL WORTH IT?

By far the two most important factors in deciding whether to attend a particular law school, or to go to law school at all, are:

(1) What sort of work are you likely to do in the first few years after you graduate?
(2) How much will it cost to get a law degree?

The answer to the first question is crucial, both because your first job or two after law school will have a very strong effect on the path the rest of your career takes, and because the further one tries to look into the future, the more difficult it becomes to predict. This is especially true in the early years of the 21st century, when the market for legal services is undergoing fundamental structural changes.

In other words, you don't want to be in a situation where you're estimating that it will take twenty or thirty years for your investment in a law degree to have produced a reasonable return. Rather, you want to be, after three or five or at the most seven years, in a position where you've earned back your initial investment, and are beginning to see a positive return on the time and money you've put into your legal career. At the very least you should by then be in a position where you can leave the practice of law – by choice or otherwise – no worse off, in economic terms, than you were before you went to law school.

After all, there is really no way to know ahead of time just how much you will or won't like being a lawyer, both because that's the kind of thing that is by nature unknowable until you actually do it, and because you can't be certain what sort of legal work you'll be in a position to do. In other words, going to law school is always a gamble. Make sure that in your case it's a calculated one.

The first calculation you need to make is how much going to law school is going to cost. Once you've determined that, you should make a realistic estimate of how much debt you'll take on over the course of law school, and how much you'll owe when your first payment becomes due six months after graduation (many prospective students fail to take into account that these two numbers are going to differ significantly).

Here's how to calculate your cost of attendance at any school you're considering:

(a) Estimate what you'll pay in tuition and fees. To do this, take the figure currently listed by the law school, add 4% to it for your second year, and 4% to that number for the third year. (For a part-time four year program add 4% to the fourth year as well).

(b) Subtract any scholarship aid from (a), discounted by the probability that you'll lose the scholarship because you fail to meet the scholarship's stipulations.

(c) Estimate your 12-month living expenses and multiply by three (four for a part-time program). Add that to the total.

(d) Subtract whatever money you and/or your family plan to contribute toward the cost of law school.

The total represents how much money you will have to borrow to get a law degree from the school you're considering. Once you have that total, add 13% if it's $75,000, 15% if it's $100,000, 17% if it's $125,000, and 18% if it's $150,000 or more. This represents the amount you will owe on your law school debt six months after graduation.

Let's work through an example. Ann plans to attend Fordham Law School in the fall of 2012. Tuition and fees are $49,500. She has been offered an annual grant of $10,000, which she will keep if she stays in good academic standing. She estimates that her 12-month cost of living, including things like books and supplies, will be $25,000 (this is a frugal figure for New York City, and Fordham is located in the most expensive part of Manhattan). Her parents have agreed to pay for half her living expenses while she is in law school and studying for the bar during the summer after graduation.

How much will Ann borrow and how much will she end up owing? Ann will be charged $124,520 in tuition: $154,520 minus $30,000 in scholarship money. The scholarship total isn't discounted in her case since she essentially can't lose it without failing out of school. If by contrast the scholarship required that she finish in the top third of the class – as scholarships at many lower-ranked law schools do – it would be worth only $10,000 total, and she would expect to pay $144,520 in tuition. *Do not attend a law school that offers you a scholarship, even a big one, subject to strict stipulations, unless you're prepared to drop out after the first year if you lose it.*

With her parents paying half her living expenses, Ann will also need to borrow $37,500 to cover the rest. Thus she estimates she will borrow $162,050 over the course of law school, rather than the $230,000 if she were paying Fordham's sticker tuition and not getting significant financial help from her family. But because interest will accrue on this total, at rates of 6.8% for the first 24,500 borrowed per year and 7.9% on the rest, Ann will owe, when her first tuition bill is due, approximately $27,540 more than she borrowed. Her debt will be

$189,600. (If she pays this debt off over ten years she will pay more than $2200 per month and a total of nearly $270,000 in principal and interest. If she opts for extended repayment and pays the debt back over 25 years she will have loan payments of $1400 and will end up paying $432,000 in principal and interest for her law degree).

Given these figures, does it make sense for Ann to attend Fordham? Answering this requires a couple of further calculations: what opportunity cost is she incurring by going to law school, and how much increased earning potential will a Fordham law degree give her? The first figure represents her estimate of what her post-tax income would be for the next three years if she were not going to law school (We will also assume she could live half as cheaply if she were not living in New York City, so the $12,500 extra her parents are paying to help cover her living expenses is also an opportunity cost of attendance, although one borne by her parents).

Ann's cost of going to law school is thus the ten or twenty-five year cost of incurring $189,600 in loans, plus the opportunity cost of not working for three years. This investment is worth incurring only if the estimated increased earning potential produced by her Fordham degree produces a positive return, over time, when compared to her true cost of attendance (the direct cost of law school, plus the cost of financing that cost, plus her opportunity cost).

Put this way the calculations sound quite technical, but they can be reduced to a pretty simple conclusion: going to Fordham is likely to make sense for Ann only if the odds are good that she can get and keep for at least several years one or more jobs that pay considerably more than the work she would do without a law degree.

At this point, Ann needs to take a very close look at Fordham's employment and salary statistics. Unfortunately Fordham has chosen to publish no salary information for its most recent graduating class. This is very concerning, given that the employment data the ABA has just begun to require the school to publish is full of serious warning signs:

(1) Despite the school's top 30 ranking, only 246 of 428 graduates in the class of 2011 had full-time long-term jobs requiring bar admission nine months after graduation.
(2) The school employed 57 of these graduates in school-funded positions, most of which were both short-term and part-time.
(3) Only a quarter of the class got big firm jobs that pay salaries which are likely to justify the investment Ann would have to make to attend the school.
(4) 52 graduates – nearly one in every eight – were completely unemployed nine months after graduation.

In short, Fordham looks like a risky bet for Ann under any circumstances, and the school will clearly be a very bad gamble if she is incurring any sort of genuine opportunity cost by attending (by, for example, leaving a stable job with even a mid-five figure salary). And of course Fordham's refusal to publish salary data for its most recent graduating class is itself a very negative sign.

What All This Means For You

Law schools – even quite high-ranked law schools – routinely charge a cost of attendance that makes a law degree a terrible and potentially life-wrecking investment for a large percentage of their graduates. To avoid being part of that percentage, you need to be coldly realistic about whether what a particular law school expects you to pay bears any reasonable relationship to the enhanced earning potential (if any) a degree from that school is likely to produce for someone in your position.

In many cases, the answer to that question is going to be "absolutely not."

10

HOW TO READ EMPLOYMENT AND SALARY STATISTICS

The good news for people considering law school is that it has become much harder for law schools to get away with reporting highly misleading employment and salary statistics. Until very recently it was common for schools to quote "employment" rates that counted every graduate who had any kind of paid work, even if that work consisted of being a part-time barista. Schools also cited "average" salary figures that didn't disclose those figures were based on absurdly small – and far from random – samples of their graduates.

Political pressure from reformers and a spate of bad media coverage have combined to finally force the ABA to require schools to publish somewhat meaningful employment statistics. You can find a version of each school's employment statistics on the ABA's website. In addition, a school should have even more detailed employment and salary numbers for its most recent classes on its own webpage (If a school doesn't publish this information in a way that allows you to fairly evaluate how well its graduates are doing, *do not apply to it*.)

Also, keep in mind that the interpretive methods schools employ when collecting employment data assume a best-case scenario when graduates provide, as they often do, incomplete information. For example if a graduate fails to indicate whether a job is long-term or short-term, a school is permitted under the ABA reporting standards to treat the job as long-term, on the basis of the assumption that most jobs for which the term of duration is reported are long-term. This means that even the fairly dire picture painted by the reported employment data systematically understates the extent of the actual crisis.

An organization called NALP publishes national employment and salary numbers, based on the data schools report to the ABA, which will give you an idea of how the market for entry-level lawyers in general looks. (About a quarter of law schools now publish the information they report to NALP on their websites). A particularly useful website for employment information is maintained by Law School Transparency, an organization founded by law students that has successfully pressured law schools to reveal more information regarding the jobs and salaries obtained by recent graduates. You should consult all these sources. After doing so, you should be able to answer the following questions:

(1) How many graduates in a school's most recent class had full-time long-term jobs requiring bar admission nine months after graduation?
(2) What kind of work did these jobs involve?
(3) How much did these jobs pay?

Again, if you can't answer all these questions fairly definitively after consulting these sources, don't consider that school. For example, any school that doesn't reveal the salary information it reports to the ABA and NALP doesn't want you to know how much its graduates are making. That by itself is a more than sufficient reason not to go to that school.

Once you find a school's statistics, here's how to read them. I'll use the school where I teach – the University of Colorado – as an example. To its credit, my school has started publishing the full data it reports to the ABA and to NALP on the school's website. But you should be able to find comparable information about any school worth considering.

CU's class of 2011 had 176 graduates. Nine months after graduation, 98 (55.7%) had full-time long-term jobs requiring bar admission (This was almost exactly the national average for ABA-accredited law schools). Let me put this as emphatically as possible: if you're considering going to law school, these are the *only* kinds of jobs you should be going to law school to get. The reason is simple: the only good reason to go to law school (assuming you're in an economic position where you have to worry about making living) is to be a lawyer.

It's true you can do a thousand things with a law degree. The problem is that you can also do 999 of those things *without* a law degree. Law school may make sense for you if you have good reasons for thinking you want to be lawyer, and you can actually become a lawyer at a reasonable cost. Otherwise, it doesn't, period. (For a fuller explanation of this, see Chapter 5).

So the first thing to note about these employment statistics is that, nine months after graduation, more than two out of five graduates didn't have what counts, under a very generous definition of the phrase, as a real legal job. (We'll see in a moment why this is such a generous definition). And keep in mind that this was at a so-called "Tier One" law school – ranked in the top quarter of all ABA schools.

The next question you should ask is: what were the people who got jobs as lawyers doing? To answer this, you need to look at how many graduates were doing legal work, even though some of these people had jobs that weren't full-time or long-term (Long-term is defined by the ABA and NALP as employment that either has no definite end date, i.e., what people think of as a "permanent" position, or that has a definite term of at least one year).

Law schools complicate their statistics by dividing jobs into several overlapping categories. This can be confusing to the prospective student. The key is to remember that, for new law graduates, there are really only three kinds of real legal jobs: working for a private law firm, working for state and local governments prosecuting crimes, and working as a public defender. (New graduates also clerk for judges, which is a temporary job that law school statistics treat as "long term." Judicial clerkships will be explained below). Yes, there are occasional exceptions. For instance, a total of 130 2011 law graduates – out of 44,495 – got jobs working for non-profit public interest law firms. Once in a great while a new law graduate manages to land a job as an in-house corporate counsel (these jobs almost always require several years of experience). Rumor has it someone was once hired straight out of law school by the Sierra Club. You're not going to be that person, so let's focus on the four kinds of legal jobs new lawyers can actually get.

When considering a law school's employment statistics, the second thing you need to do, after figuring out how many graduates had, nine months after graduation, real legal jobs, broadly defined (that is, full-time long term positions requiring bar admission), is to figure out how many graduates were doing the four kinds of legal jobs that a new law graduate can realistically hope to have a chance to get. If you can't figure this information out from the school's web site, ask the school for a copy of its most recent NALP report. If the school won't give you one, eliminate it from consideration. Plenty of law schools publish this information: those that don't are trying to take your money without giving you the facts you need to make an informed choice. Don't give it to them.

So: 65 grads from the CU class of 2011 were working for law firms. 38 were clerking for judges. Six were working as prosecutors. Two were public defenders. The next step is to break down the specific kinds of jobs people had in each of these categories. Law firm jobs can be divided into three basic types: small firms, medium-sized firms, and large firms. Small firms have no more than ten attorneys. Medium-sized firms employ 11 to 100 attorneys. Big firms feature more than 100 attorneys (Obviously these are rough categories, but they're useful for getting a quick snapshot of what a school's graduates do in their first legal jobs. As we will see, a graduate's first job out of law school tends to have a very strong effect on the graduate's future path inside the legal profession).

With occasional exceptions, the bigger a firm is, the more it pays, and the more options it creates in terms of future legal employment. So a crucial piece of information for any prospective law student is, how many of a school's graduates get jobs with firms of various sizes. In the CU class of 2011, 30 graduates took jobs with small firms, 26 with medium-sized firms, and eight with large firms. (This particular piece of information is available for every school on the ABA's website, but if a school doesn't also make it available on its own website, that's a red flag).

Judicial clerkships are of two types: clerkships with federal and with state judges. With rare exceptions, they usually last for exactly one year, and therefore count as "long-term" employment in law school statistics, although they aren't long-term jobs in the ordinary sense. Federal clerkships are considered quite prestigious, and are often – although less so than in the past – a stepping stone to high-status legal employment. State and local clerkships make up a much more ambiguous and problematic category. A few such clerkships – for state supreme court justices – can be nearly as desirable as federal clerkships, in terms of future employment opportunities (Remember, clerkships only last for one year, so the question of what sort of employment opportunities they create is crucial). But most state and local clerkships tend to provide only a minimal boost to a graduate's post-clerkship job prospects. (If you look at the statistics for the most elite law schools – Yale, Stanford, and Harvard – almost none of their graduates end up in anything other than federal or state supreme court clerkships).

In sum, federal clerkships should be considered a real positive when evaluating a school's employment statistics, while a large number of state clerkships is at best a neutral indicator, and quite often a warning sign that many of the school's graduates couldn't get minimally acceptable, genuinely long-term legal jobs. Eight members of the CU class of 2011 secured federal clerkships, while 30 went into state clerkship positions. (In the ABA statistics, available on the ABA's webpage, federal clerkships make up the category called "Federal," while state and local clerkships make up the category "State and Local." Again, a school's own website ought to include this information, and schools which don't include it, or worse yet list "clerkships" without differentiating between different types, should be treated with suspicion).

When it comes to prosecutor and public defender jobs, the ABA statistics are unfortunately quite vague. Prosecutor positions are included in the general category of "government" jobs, which include all government employment (other than public defender positions) whether the job in question requires a law degree or not (I recently encountered a graduate who had gone to law school after spending a decade as a mail carrier. After being unable to get a job as a lawyer he returned to his mail route. He counted as employed by the government in the ABA and NALP statistics.).

In the ABA statistics, public defenders are included in the larger public interest category, which has come to include large numbers of people "interning" – this means working for free – or filling short-term positions, often funded by law schools, who create short-term jobs for their graduates to artificially pump up the schools' employment rates. (The ABA statistics do reveal how many graduates are in law-school funded jobs. You should simply subtract all these jobs from the school's purported employment rate).

Law schools know how many of their graduates in "government" and "public interest" positions have jobs as prosecutors and public defenders, and you should insist, politely but firmly, that they reveal this information if it's not available on their websites, by giving you a copy of their most recent NALP reports. This is especially the case, of course, if you think you may want to do this type of work.

There's a lot of noise in law school employment statistics, and the best way to avoid being misled is to focus exclusively on the categories that are made up of the kinds of legal jobs new lawyers can get. This means you should ignore the "business and industry" and "academia" categories, which with occasional exceptions are made up of jobs people could have gotten without going to law school, or, in the case of "academia," usually consist of short-term law school-funded jobs.

Once you've determined what percentage of a law school's graduates are getting real legal jobs, generously defined, and what those jobs involve doing, you should turn to the school's salary data. Here the ABA statistics are of no direct use: the ABA's Section of Legal Education, which is largely controlled by deans from low-ranked schools with terrible employment outcomes, has managed to this point to successfully resist demands that it use its regulatory power to force schools to reveal salary data.

Here again you should employ a bright line rule: Do not consider applying to any school that does not publish reasonably comprehensive data regarding the salaries obtained by its graduates. "Reasonably comprehensive" means the following: the school must reveal the *percentage of the graduates in a class* for which it has such data, along with the distribution of salaries in terms of medians, means, and percentiles.

Not long ago, law schools either published no salary data at all, or published egregiously misleading figures, which they failed to reveal were based on a small minority of their graduates. Due to pressure from the law school reform movement, the situation has improved markedly in just the last year or two, but a significant number of schools still refuse to disclose meaningful salary data. Anyone who at this point applies to such a school is engaging in frankly reckless behavior. So don't.

Here is the salary data for the CU class of 2011. The school managed to obtain salary information regarding 100 of 176 graduates. The median salary for the graduates who had a known salary was $53,000. The 25th percentile was $46,000 and the 75th percentile was $70,000. Thirteen graduates (7.4%) had a salary of $100,000 or more. All this information is available on the school's web site. If you can't find salary information at a similar level of detail on the website of a school you're considering, ask for the school's NALP report. (Let the school know that you will not consider applying without this information).

Of course it's reasonable to assume that the salary outcomes for graduates whose salary is unknown are in all likelihood considerably worse than those of graduates whose salaries are known. A consistent pattern in the salary data is that people with high salaries tend to report them, while people with low or non-existent salaries are much less likely to do so. For example in 2011 the salaries of 93% of graduates who got jobs with large law firms were obtained by law schools, compared to 40% of graduates who were employed by small law firms. A rule of thumb: the smaller the percentage of graduates for whom a school has salary information is, the less you should be willing to consider applying to that school.

Summing up, courtesy of the ABA you can now find the percentage of any law school's most recent graduating class who obtained full-time "long-term" employment requiring bar admission. But this should be only the beginning of your research regarding the employment and salary outcomes enjoyed by a school's graduates. If, after studying the information the school makes public, you're still unclear regarding just what sorts of legal jobs its graduates are working at, and/or how much those jobs pay, ask the school for its most recent NALP report. Given the cost of law school, and the state of the employment market for lawyers, there is simply no excuse for any school failing to disclose to prospective students exactly the same employment and salary information it reports to NALP.

What All This Means For You

Here's a simple rule: if a school won't share some piece of information you need to help you understand what its graduates end up doing, and how much they're paid to do it, don't apply. Remember, these days almost all law schools need your money and your LSAT/GPA numbers more than you need the degrees they offer. Don't assume they're doing you a favor by admitting you: they're not. You're doing them a favor when and if you choose to accept their offers of admission. Any school that acts as if it doesn't understand that isn't worth either your money or your time.

11

HOW TO PICK A LAW SCHOOL

Picking a law school to attend requires taking three basic steps:

(1) First, you need to determine what kind of job you're going to law school in order to get, and what your backup plan is if you don't get that kind of job.
(2) Second, you need to determine what the odds are that you will be able to get the kind of job you want to get if you attend a particular school.
(3) Third, you need to determine how much it will cost to attend a particular school, in order to decide if going to that school makes financial sense, given the odds of getting the kind of job you're going to law school to try to get.

Going to law school only makes sense if you want to be a lawyer. (The line law schools try to push that a law degree is "versatile" is dangerous nonsense. See Chapter 5). There are, from the perspective of the new law school grad, three kinds of jobs for lawyers: working for a law firm, working as a prosecutor, and working as a public defender. (It's true that lawyers do other things, such as work in-house for corporations, but such jobs are almost never available to new law school graduates. New graduates also clerk for judges. See Chapter 10 on how judicial clerkships should be taken into account).

You should only go to law school if you have some reasonable basis for believing you actually want to do at least one of these three things. In addition, you should ideally have some realistic backup plan if your first choice doesn't work out.

Having a reasonable basis for believing you want to do some type of work requires having some real idea of what that type of work involves. You should only consider going to law school if you've made a genuine effort to get some sense of what working in various legal jobs is really like (watching TV shows about lawyers doesn't count). For instance, if you think you want to be a prosecutor, you should have interned at a district attorney's office during college. If you want to work as a public defender, you should do the same somewhere in your local public defender system. If you think you want to work for a big law firm, try to get some sort of staff position at such a firm, so you can at least get a second-hand glimpse of what lawyers at these firms do.

In any case, you should treat one rule as ironclad: absolutely *do not* go to law school as a default career decision, because you can't think of what else to do. A generation ago drifting into the legal profession was a bad idea: today, it's a prescription for economic and emotional disaster.

Once you have a reasonable basis for knowing why you want to go to law school, you need to decide where to apply. The fundamental problem with the economics of legal education in America today is that an investment in a law degree only makes sense under one of two scenarios: If the graduate gets a high-paying job with a big law firm, or if the graduate is attending law school at a very heavily discounted price. (I'm ignoring two fairly unusual types of applicants: people from very wealthy backgrounds who are going to law school as a form of conspicuous consumption, in the same way fifty years ago Ivy League colleges were largely finishing schools for the social elites, and people who already have a legal job waiting for them, for example with their family's firm, and merely need the credential).

What this means is that most people currently attending law school would be better off not doing so. This is a harsh truth, but if you want to play the law school game successfully, it's essential to understand it.

Let's consider the case of Alex. Alex has been a paralegal at a big national law firm for the past two years, and he wants to go to law school in order to work as a lawyer at such a firm. After a few years in big law he sees himself either moving to a smaller but still fairly large regional firm, or getting a job in-house with the legal department of one of the national firm's clients. Alex is realistic about the fact that becoming an equity partner at a big national firm is a very long shot for any prospective law student, and no one should go to law school in the expectation that he or she will end up in such a position.

Alex's backup plan, if he doesn't get a high-paying big law firm job, is to either graduate from a school that has a generous loan repayment assistance program (LRAP), or to graduate with a small enough amount of debt that taking a low-paying job with small firm will not be a financial disaster.

What law schools should Alex consider? The answer is that there are very few schools – really no more than a dozen or so – that he ought to consider attending at anything close to full price. After all, in 2011 only 11 law schools sent as many as 35% of their graduates to law firms of more than 100 lawyers (this category includes almost all the law firm jobs in the United States that pay six-figure starting salaries). Now this somewhat understates the chances of a graduate from such schools getting a job with a big firm, as we can assume that most graduates who obtain federal judicial clerkships could get such a job. In addition we can estimate that perhaps five to ten percent of the students at elite law schools are what can be called "public interest dedicated" – that is, people who have no intention of getting a big firm job, even for a few years, because they are dedicated to trying to obtain a job in the public sector.

But even making these allowances, there were in 2011 perhaps 12 to 15 law schools – out of 201 ABA-accredited institutions – where we can say with confidence that at least half the graduates who wanted big law firm jobs got them. And if we drop that number to one third – that is, schools that gave graduates who wanted big law at least a one in three chance of success – the total number of schools only grows to about 25. (See Chapter 10 for a guide to how to determine what a school's actual placement numbers look like).

What about Alex's backup plan? Not surprisingly, the schools with generous LRAP programs make up a subset of the schools that would give him at least a 50/50 chance of obtaining a job with a large law firm. (The vast majority of law schools don't have the resources to provide much more than token loan repayment assistance to a few of their graduates, if that. And even most of the very few schools with substantial LRAP programs are now scaling them back. See Chapter 8).

Given his career goals, Alex should consider only two types of law schools:

(1) The handful of elite national schools that will give him a realistic chance to obtain a big law job; or

(2) A high-quality regional law school that sends more than a trivial number of graduates to big law firms, *as long as* – these caveats are crucial – this school offers Alex a very large discount on tuition, and Alex has ties to the area where the school is located.

Let's explore the second category of schools in more detail. The vast majority of law schools send less than ten percent of their graduates to big law firms. Alex should not consider any of these schools, even if they offer him full tuition scholarships. It's simply a bad gamble to incur three years of opportunity costs, and end up borrowing $50,000 or more in living expenses, for a less than ten to one shot at the kind of job Alex is going to law school to get. Furthermore schools that place trivial numbers of students with big law firms also tend to have high percentages of truly disastrous outcomes for their graduates, such as not being able to obtain any kind of legal job at all, or complete unemployment.

The non-elite schools Alex should consider are places that send a combined total of 15% to 30% of their graduates to big law firms or federal judicial clerkships, and that also offer him very large tuition discounts, so that he can expect to graduate with considerably less than $100,000 in law school debt. In addition, however, Alex should have some connection to the area in which a school in this category is located: he should not, for example, move to Boston to attend Boston College if he does not have a pre-existing reason for wanting to work in the Boston area.

The reason pre-existing connections are so important is that, with the exception of the handful of truly national law schools, law school hiring tends to be highly regional. Roughly one quarter of the class at Boston College can expect to be offered jobs with large law firms, but most of those jobs will be with Boston-area firms. Not surprisingly, those firms look favorably on candidates that have both high law school grades and pre-existing connections to the Boston area. Because law firms need to train their associates, they are leery of hiring someone who is at a higher risk, all things being equal, to leave for another job within a year or two of being hired.

Of course this preference isn't set in stone: good regional law firms do sometimes hire people with no pre-existing connections to the area, if they are otherwise outstanding candidates. But for someone who wants to get into big law, not being from the area where a school is located is a significant negative – unless, of course, the student is attending an elite national law school.

Given that, all things being equal, Alex is already looking at no better than a one in four chance of getting the kind of job he wants if he attends a school like Boston College, he should only attend this type of school if the regional nature of the school is working in his favor, rather than against him.

How much should Alex be willing to pay to attend a highly-ranked regional school, which sends a non-trivial number of its graduates to large law firms? If Alex is getting no family support to help pay for law school, he should be unwilling to pay much more than $10,000 per year in tuition to attend such a school. Any more than that will, considering the cost of living, leave him with six figures of law school debt, which is too great of a risk to take on, given the odds are against him getting a big firm job with a degree from such a school.

Now let's consider the case of Emily. Emily is going to law school because she wants to be a prosecutor. She has no interest in working for a private law firm, so her backup plan, if she is unable to secure a job with a district attorney's office, is to get some other sort of government or public interest legal job. Because Emily's career choices involve jobs that pay salaries that will not allow her to service the debt she would incur by attending almost any law school, and certainly no private law school, at anything approaching full price, the factors that Emily should take into account in regard to potential law schools will be somewhat different than Alex's.

Because government and public interest law hiring is (relatively) less status-driven than big firm hiring, Emily has in one sense a potentially broader array of law schools she may wish to consider than Alex, who should only consider the small minority of law schools that send more than a tiny percentage of their graduates to large law firms. But in another sense Emily's choices are more constrained: if, like Alex, she is largely or wholly paying for the cost of law school herself, she will not be able to reasonably afford what today is considered even a moderate amount of law school debt.

Emily should not take on more than $50,000 in debt to attend law school, unless she is fortunate enough to get into one of the tiny group of schools that feature generous LRAP programs. Otherwise, she should not attend law school unless she receives a full tuition scholarship, or something very close to that.

In addition, before enrolling in law school, Emily should take into account that legal jobs in the public sector are becoming ever-more competitive, and that public employers are increasingly willing to consider applications only from people whose background both before and during law school indicates they are "public law committed" – that is, people whose resumes demonstrate that they aren't treating public law as some sort of backup plan (At present, even people with high grades from elite schools find it difficult or impossible to get public sector jobs if they don't have the appropriate prior background).

Emily should consider schools that place more than a handful of their graduates in positions with prosecutors' offices, and other government and public interest legal jobs. Note the large majority of law schools will fail to meet this criterion. (Chapter 10 discusses how to interpret law school employment data. Again, *do not apply* to any school that will not disclose the data you need to evaluate your prospects of successful employment adequately). Emily should narrow her consideration to schools which have respectable placement numbers in her areas of interest, and which she can attend on something approaching a full scholarship (with an exception for the tiny group of elite schools with well-funded LRAP programs).

Of course there's no way for Alex and Emily to know in advance whether they will admitted to the right sorts of law schools, and be offered enough money to attend them, given their career goals. In fact there's a very good chance they won't be (This is just another way of saying that, under current conditions, law school will end up being a bad choice for the large majority of people who go).

What is absolutely critical for both Alex and Emily, before they embark on the law school application process, is to commit themselves to refusing to enroll at any law school that does not offer them a combination of career prospects and cost of attendance that would make it sensible for them to attend. This means that, in all likelihood, it will be best for them not apply at all, once they have enough information to judge where they're likely to be accepted.

In the alternative, if their application profiles are strong enough that they're among the minority of applicants for who pursuing admission to law school continues to make sense, it's imperative that they take a very hard line when they negotiate scholarship offers with the schools that admit them. Alex and Emily both need to tell law schools in no uncertain terms how much money they're willing to pay in tuition, given the relationship between their career goals, their cost of attendance, and the probability that they will be able to achieve those goals by attending the schools they're considering.

In this context, it's crucial to keep in mind that, especially under current circumstances, law schools need applicants to accept offers of admission far more than applicants need those offers. To put it bluntly, if a law school tells you it is out of "scholarship" money, that school is lying to you. Remember, what law schools call "scholarships" are nothing but discounts on the advertised price of tuition. If a law school refuses to discount tuition to a level that's acceptable to you, the school is simply holding out in a negotiation over price. And the key to winning any such negotiation is to always be ready to walk away.

What All This Means For You

Given the current price of law school, and the odds of securing the kinds of jobs that would justify paying what most law students are paying to get a law degree, the large majority of current law students should not be attending the schools they're attending at the price they're paying for attending them. For them, law school is likely to be a losing game.

In order to avoid being one of these students, you need to be clear on what kind of job you would go to law school to get, what the odds are that you'll get that job if you graduate from a particular school, and how much it makes sense to pay to go to that school, given those odds. Keep in mind that, given the current state of legal academia and the job market for lawyers, there's a very good chance that it will end up not making sense for you to go to law school. To increase your odds of winning this game, you need to be willing not to play it.

12

WHY RANKINGS DON'T MATTER

Law schools obsess over law school rankings, and most especially the rankings put out by *U.S. News & World Report*, the rump internet survivor of a defunct print news magazine. Every year a law school dean or two gets the axe because his or her school slipped a few notches in the rankings, and every year schools come up with ever-more creative ways to play the rankings game, in an attempt to move up – or at least not fall – from their present position.

Schools rationalize this behavior by pointing out that prospective law students use the rankings to help them decide which schools to consider, and where to enroll if and when they receive multiple acceptances.

For both law schools and prospective students it's a bizarre and wasteful game, and you shouldn't play it. Here's why: rankings don't matter.

This is an overstatement, but far closer to the truth than the behavior of schools and applicants would lead you to believe. *Rankings only matter to the extent they reflect significant differences in employment outcomes for graduates.* To the (often very great) extent law school rankings don't reflect such differences, they should be ignored. In this sense, it "matters" that third-ranked Harvard is ranked ahead of sixth-ranked New York University, even though both are elite law school by any reasonable definition, because Harvard graduates experience significantly better employment outcomes than NYU graduates.

By contrast, the fact that Minnesota was ranked 19th nationally in 2011 while Southern Methodist was ranked 51st – a gap that both the schools themselves and many applicants would consider enormously important – dwindles to irrelevance given another fact: by every reasonable measure SMU graduates the previous year had as good or better employment outcomes than Minnesota graduates.

The rankings themselves are constructed using a farcical method that takes into account all sorts of meaningless and even counterproductive information. The best example of this is that *US News* treats expenditures per student as a proxy for quality – which means that if School A and School B are identical in every respect, except that School A charges higher tuition that School B, School A will be ranked higher! Of course this is an incentive to law schools to engage massively inefficient spending, and they have proceeded to do so.

Until recently, prospective students were more or less forced to give the rankings far more attention than they ever deserved, because very little in the way of reliable information was available regarding employment and salary outcomes for graduates of individual law schools. The information schools publicized was often wildly misleading: schools made no distinction between legal and non-legal jobs when reporting employment rates, and didn't reveal that "average" salary numbers were often based on small and completely unrepresentative samples of graduates.

This situation is changing rapidly: prospective students can look up what percentage of a school's graduating class got full-time long-term jobs requiring bar admission, how many got jobs with law firms of various sizes, how many got public interest positions, and other information as well. Reliable salary data is not as widely available, because the ABA has yet to require schools to make it public, but pressure from reformers has led to many schools publishing fairly comprehensive salary data, and you should absolutely refuse to consider any school that does not reveal, at a minimum, the percentage of their graduates for whom they have salary information, and the mean and median salaries of graduates in various practice settings.

Now that the basic employment and salary information is available from any school that's worth considering, there is no reason whatsoever to pay attention to the rankings themselves. And what that information reveals is how severe the gap is in regard to employment outcomes between a handful of elite schools and everyone else.

Keep in mind that the only job track that pays enough to justify what is now the cost of law school for most law students is to either get a job with a big law firm upon graduation, or to secure a federal judicial clerkship and then go on to such a job (The assumption, which used to be a fairly safe one, that anyone with a federal clerkship could get a big firm job, is becoming increasingly questionable, but for the purposes of this analysis I'm going to treat it as valid).

If you look at the statistics for the class of 2011, you'll find that only ten of 201 ABA law schools had as many as half their graduating class go to either big firms – those with more than 100 attorneys – or federal clerkships, combined. And the drop off from that point is truly extreme: only eight more schools sent as many of a quarter of their graduates to such jobs. *The large majority of law schools sent less than ten percent of their graduating classes to big firm jobs and federal clerkships, combined.*

It's true there are other in some ways desirable legal jobs available for entry level lawyers, such as working for state and federal governments, or as public defenders, or for public interest law firms. But remember: such jobs do not pay nearly enough to service the debt that will be acquired by anyone who borrows anything close to the average cost of attendance at the typical law school. This means that, if you are fortunate enough to get such a job, you will have to depend on the government's Public Service Loan Forgiveness (PSLF) program to forgive the remainder of your debt after ten years of reduced-rate loan payments.

This in turn requires holding onto a government or public interest job for ten years, and carrying a large and growing unsecured debt load for a decade – something that could well interfere with securing home mortgages, car loans, and other forms of consumer credit. (Such a career plan also requires depending on the federal government not to eliminate the PSLF program before your debt is paid off).

A bigger problem with government and public interest jobs, from the perspective of the someone considering law school, is that a combination of factors are making such jobs very difficult to secure – often even more difficult than positions with big firms. These include employment freezes and layoffs throughout the public sector, and the increasing unwillingness of lawyers who already have such jobs to leave them, given the advantages they provide in regard to debt forgiveness. (Another factor that makes these jobs difficult to get is the relative desirability of the kind of work public lawyers do, compared to the sort of work that would be available to them in the private sector).

Again, the only two things you should take into account when considering a law school are employment outcomes, and cost. Employment outcomes bear only a loose relationship to rankings: currently a handful of elite schools have good employment outcomes, a couple of dozen other schools have mediocre employment outcomes, and the vast majority of law schools have employment outcomes that in no way come close to justifying their cost of attendance. As for the cost of attendance, it bears an even looser relation to rankings: while all elite schools are now extremely expensive, most non-elite schools are, with a shrinking number of exceptions, not much if at all cheaper.

For years, the *U.S. News* rankings have had a terrible effect on legal education, as schools have wasted untold sums of student tuition money trying to improve their relative position in this preposterous system of pseudo-evaluation. The rankings were considered important because schools managed to avoid disclosing meaningful employment and salary data: data which, if they had been disclosed, would have revealed that schools were charging far more for law degrees than those degrees were worth.

Luckily, there's quite a bit of evidence that, as employment and salary data become available, prospective law students are coming to realize that the rankings themselves are almost meaningless, except as often inaccurate proxies for information that can now finally be accessed directly. From the perspective of the law school reform movement, this is a very positive development. The less attention prospective students give to rankings, the less excuse law schools will have to waste their students' money playing this wasteful and ridiculous game that, over the past 25 years, has come to have such an invidious influence on the decisions law schools and law students make.

What All This Means For You

In the brave new world of relatively transparent employment and salary information, law school rankings mean next to nothing. What prospective students are discovering is that being a "top tier" or even "top 20" law school in no way guarantees that an acceptable percentage of the school's graduates will end up in legal jobs that come close to justifying the cost of attendance, or indeed will necessarily get legal jobs at all. Smart and well-informed people now pay no attention to the rankings when considering and comparing law schools. They pay attention to two things: attendance costs and employment outcomes. Make sure that you do the same.

13

THE TRANSFER GAME

As the dire employment and salary figures for law graduates in general, and for the graduates of lower-ranked schools in particular, become better known, prospective law students are increasingly prone to rationalize their enrollment decisions by telling themselves that they'll transfer to a better school after their first year.

This has always been a dangerous line of thinking. Indeed, somewhat counter-intuitively, it's getting even more dangerous now, as transferring from a lower to a higher ranked school is getting easier to do. This chapter is about is about the transfer game: how to play it, and the traps to look out for, if you're looking to trade up in the law school world.

The first thing to understand about transferring after your first year is that different law schools have very different policies in regard to how many transfer students they'll take. Some high-ranked schools, such as for example Duke and Texas, tend to take very few transfer students (they took seven and six transfer students respectively in 2011), while others take huge numbers of transferees. For instance in 2011 Georgetown and George Washington admitted a combined total of 175 transfer students. (Last year more than 20% of George Washington's second and third year classes were made up of students who had spent their first year of law school elsewhere).

If you're a first-year student who is thinking about transferring, LSAC's *Guide to ABA Law Schools* has the numbers regarding how many students transferred into and out of each ABA school. On the other hand, if you're a prospective law student who is thinking about going to a particular school and then transferring after your first year, you need a different plan. Here's why:

(1) Transferring remains difficult to do. It's far easier to get a higher score on an LSAT retake than it is to finish in the top ten percent of a law school class, which is probably what you'll have to do to have a chance to transfer to any school into which it's worth transferring. (If you're at a third-tier or unranked school, you may well have to finish in the top five percent).

(2) Transfer students can be at a disadvantage when it comes to on campus interviewing at their new school. (Remember, the OCI process takes place at the beginning of your second year, and at that point your entire law school academic record consists of your first year grades). For one thing, many firms will interview transfer students on the same basis that they would interview the student at the student's original school, which is to say that if the firm never hires people from the Diploma Mill School of Law, it probably won't consider hiring you just because you're at Georgetown now.

(3) The most problematic aspect of transferring for most students who consider it is the financial cost. Transfer candidates are often people with strong initial law school entrance qualifications, who took large scholarships to attend lower ranked schools, rather than paying full price at higher ranked ones. Transfer students usually end up paying the advertised full sticker price at their new schools (Although as high-ranked schools come under increasing pressure to enroll highly qualified applicants from a shrinking overall applicant pool, they are starting to offer "scholarship" money to transfers).

All of which is to say that a first-year law student should think very carefully about whether increasing the cost of law school is worth whatever benefit the student is likely to get from transferring to a higher ranked school. And prospective law students should never consider the possibility of transferring when evaluating whether attending a particular school at a certain price is likely to be a good investment.

Consider Michael's case. Michael has just finished his first year at Michigan State's law school, with grades in the top 5% of the class. He has an opportunity to transfer to George Washington. He would like to get a job with a good-sized law firm, yet less than five percent (13 of 283) 2011 graduates of MSU obtained a job with law firm of more than 50 attorneys. Meanwhile 23% (120 of 518) George Washington's 2011 graduates got such jobs.

This would seem like an easy decision – until we start analyzing the finances of this decision. Michael has a 50% tuition scholarship, which means he can anticipate paying about $39,000 total tuition for his remaining two years of law school if he stays at MSU. If he transfers to George Washington, he can expect to pay nearly $100,000 – $60,000 more. The cost of living is also much higher in Washington than in East Lansing, so transferring to George Washington is going to increase the total cost of attendance for Michael's last two years of law school by, conservatively, $75,000.

And keep in mind that it's far from clear that transferring will actually increase Michael's chances of getting a job with a large law firm. After all, he is near the top of the class at MSU, and while very few MSU students get such jobs, he can reasonably assume that his grades make him a good candidate to be one of them. Meanwhile, he can only take an educated guess regarding how employers at George Washington's fall OCI will view his Michigan State transcript. Will they consider him equivalent to someone who finished in the top ten percent of the class as a first-year at George Washington, or the top 20%, or the top third? It's difficult to say. Some firms – those that never interview at schools equivalent to Michigan State – will not consider him at all.

So while it's true that in general it's far easier – although still quite difficult – for George Washington students to get jobs with big firms than it is for Michigan State students, it's not obvious that Michael will improve his career prospects by transferring. What is clear is that this move would cost him a very large sum of money, which he will probably borrow, and on which interest will start accruing as soon as he borrows it, so that this extra $75,000 will be an extra $85,000 by the time he takes the bar.

What Michael should certainly do is go to MSU's administration, tell the school he's seriously considering transferring, and ask the school to increase his scholarship. The flip side of the transfer game is that lower-ranked schools are becoming ever-more desperate to hold onto those few of their students who have a reasonable chance of securing high-paying jobs. If Michael gets such a job, that could well, in the eyes of the school, be worth more to MSU than the extra ten or twenty thousand dollars of "scholarship" money it would cost them to keep him from transferring.

What All This Means For You

Transferring to higher-ranked law schools is becoming both easier and more potentially dangerous for top students at low-ranked schools. It's becoming easier for the same reason it's becoming more dangerous: because the employment statistics at many high-ranked schools are getting bad enough that the potential benefit from being a transfer student at a high-ranked school, as opposed to a top student at a low-ranked school, is becoming increasingly unclear. This is especially true when you take into account that any top-ranked student a lower-ranked school should be able to arrange to pay very little or no tuition for the last two years of law school, while transferring to a high-ranked school will almost certainly mean paying a huge two-year tuition bill at an extremely expensive (and seriously overpriced) institution.

Under no circumstances should you enroll at a low-ranked school while planning to transfer after your first year. Law school grades are far too unpredictable to make such a plan anything but a prescription for serious disappointment, if not outright disaster.

14

KNOWING WHEN TO QUIT

The most important thing for any prospective law student to keep in mind is that, at present, the large majority of law graduates – perhaps 80% – end up *worse off* after going to law school than they were before they enrolled. For these graduates, their law degrees have what economists refer to as "negative net present value." This is a fancy way of saying they paid too much to try to become lawyers, given what their long-term career prospects ended up looking like after graduation. In other words, most law students today should not be going to law school.

How can you avoid joining this group? The first step is to be clear on exactly why you're going to law school, and how much it makes sense to pay to go, given your goals and the probability of achieving them. Once you examine the relevant data in regard to these considerations, you'll discover that law schools fall into three categories:

(1) Schools that it would be worth it for you to attend at the advertised sticker price. This will be a very small category.
(2) Schools that it would be worth it for you to attend at a heavily discounted price, or for "free" (meaning on a full-tuition scholarship). This is a larger category, but one that will still include only a minority of all law schools.

(3) Schools that would be a bad investment, given your career goals, even if you could attend them without paying any tuition at all. This category will probably end up including most ABA-accredited schools.

Before applying to law school, you need to be ruthlessly realistic with yourself: Given you admission numbers – which is to say your undergraduate GPA and your best LSAT score – how likely is that you'll gain admission to a school in category (1), or, alternatively, a school in category (2) at a sufficiently discounted price? To help you answer these questions go to the website Law School Numbers (www.lawschoolnumbers.com).

There, you will be able to see what your chances of admission are to various schools, and, just as important, how much "scholarship" money – that is, how big of a tuition discount – you can expect to be offered by schools that are likely to admit you. Keep in mind that an important consideration in this regard is whether or not an applicant is an Under-Represented Minority (URM). This will usually, but not always, be noted in an applicant's LSN profile. URMs will be admitted to much better schools than non-URM candidates with similar numbers.

Once you've made this initial analysis, you should have a very good idea of whether you're likely to be admitted to a school worth attending, given your career goals, at a price worth paying. It is absolutely imperative to keep in mind that, for the vast majority of potential law school applicants, the answer to this question will be an unambiguous "no."

If you should find yourself in this category – and again the odds are strong that you will – you should do one of two things:

(1) Forget about law school; or
(2) Retake the LSAT.

What you should *not* do is apply to law school and hope that somehow you'll be admitted to a law school it makes sense for you to attend at a price it makes sense for you to pay. The odds of this happening are far lower than the odds that you will, against your better judgment, end up attending a school you shouldn't attend, once the inertial forces of the law school application process have taken over.

If it's unlikely you'll get into a law school that's worth your money and time, and you still think you want to become a lawyer, retake the LSAT. The LSAT is a learnable test, and there are several good guidebooks available that will help you figure out how to maximize your score (There is plenty of valuable advice on this topic on the internet. Be wary of big commercial test preparation companies, however). LSAC, the organization that administers the LSAT, allows people to take the test as many as three times within a two-year period. If your first LSAT score doesn't give you the numbers you need to get into a law school that's worth attending, trying to improve your score significantly is a far better strategy than "planning" to finish in the top 10% of the class, and/or transferring to a better school after your first year. (The latter plans are recipes for disaster).

Throughout this process one psychological trap that you should try very hard to avoid is the sunk cost fallacy (As we will see this becomes an even more crucial consideration once someone actually starts attending law school). The sunk cost fallacy is the name economists and psychologists give to the following tendency: Suppose you are playing poker. Your initial position in a hand looks strong, so you make a big bet. As play progresses – more cards are drawn or revealed – your position suddenly looks much weaker. When deciding whether to bet yet more money or fold, it's an almost universal human tendency to take into account how much money you've put into the pot already. But a good poker player doesn't do this, because he understands the money he put into the pot no longer belongs to him. He will only stay in the hand if his calculation of the expected return on investing yet more money into the pot is positive. If not, then the smart move is to fold and cut his losses. To do otherwise is to, as the expression goes, "throw good money after bad."

Here's another example: Suppose you buy a stock at $30 per share, and two years later it is at $15. The price at which you bought the stock is (tax considerations aside) simply irrelevant to the question of whether selling it now rather than holding onto it is the better investment decision going forward. The money you paid for the stock two years ago, like the money you initially bet early in the poker hand, is a sunk cost: that money has already been spent, and the only relevant question is whether in your estimate the stock is a good investment for the future at its present price of $15 per share.

The sunk cost fallacy is extremely powerful and difficult to combat. Thus prospective law students who have spent two years and a couple of thousand dollars trying to improve their LSAT scores are tempted to apply, even when they're practically certain not to get into a law school worth going to at a price worth paying, because otherwise they believe that time and money will have been "wasted." This is an understandable state of mind, but the fact that it's understandable doesn't make it rational. The time and money spent trying to make law school a good gamble are gone: they're sunk costs, and therefore irrelevant to the question of whether spending that time and money has in fact ended up making law school a worthwhile gamble for the prospective applicant.

The sunk cost fallacy can do even more damage during law school itself. Once a prospective student has taken the plunge and actually enrolled, knowing when to quit can become an issue of overriding importance. Let us return to Alex, the prospective law student who in Chapter 11 was trying to determine what law schools it might make sense for him to attend, and at what price.

Suppose Alex ended up enrolling at a good regional law school, which sends about a quarter of the class to the sorts of large law firms where he hoped to get a job. Alex enrolled in this school in part because he negotiated a large scholarship, so after his first year he has taken out $12,000 in loans for tuition, and another $15,000 for living expenses. By early June he has gotten all of his first-year grades, which put him in approximately the middle of his class. Alex has been unable to get paid legal work for the summer, and he faces a decision: should he continue with law school?

The hard truth is that, every year, thousands of law students face, or ought to face, the same question. Those who approach the matter in the right way will understand that, under present conditions, law school is a calculated high stakes gamble. First-year grades are the equivalent of seeing the flop – the first three of five community cards – in Texas hold 'em. For many of the players at the table, the smart move at this point in the game is to fold. (First-year law school grades are by far the most important grades a student will receive, because they determine whether a student has any chance of getting a job through on-campus interviewing during the fall of the student's second year. Almost all jobs with large law firms are secured by second-year students interviewing at OCI).

Alex's $27,000 in loans are the equivalent of the first round of betting. In other words, that money is gone. That he has spent it has no relevance to the question of whether he ought to borrow another $60,000 to get a law degree, given that his chances of getting the kind of job he went to law school to try to get have now become very slim.

Should Alex continue to try to play what's looking like a busted hand? The question doesn't necessarily have an easy answer, but law schools work hard to try to ensure that people in Alex's position never even ask it. (If they did, the answers would have dire consequences for law school budgets).

The disturbing reality is that many current law students lost the law school game even before they enrolled, and many others ought to drop out after their first year. If you end up deciding to go to law school, you should do so while retaining a genuine option, in your own mind and by the manner in which you present the decision to others, to drop out should circumstances warrant it. Indeed, given the state of the legal market, *most people at most law schools who find themselves in the bottom half of the class after their first year would be better off dropping out.*

The point is that after the first year you will have much more information about whether your initial calculated gamble seems likely to pan out. You will have your most important grades; you will have at least a slightly better idea of whether you're likely to find some type of legal work enjoyable or at least tolerable; and you may have an improved sense of what job prospects will end up looking like for people in your position (Abstract statistics, while crucial, can't reveal every relevant variable).

Again, one thing that should not affect your decision is that you've invested time and money in law school, any more than the fact you invested time and money applying to law school ought to have affected your ultimate decision to enroll. Your first year in law school is a sunk cost. Whether you should drop out (more precisely, whether you should take a leave of absence, which gives you the option to return) is a question whose answer shouldn't be affected by that cost.

What should determine that decision are the answers to the same questions you should ask before enrolling in law school in the first place: how much is this going to cost *going forward*, and what are the odds that you will experience an outcome that will justify that cost? Nine months after your first day of classes, you will have far more information relevant to the second question than you had on that first day. Don't be afraid to use that information to your benefit. Remember, the point of folding a bad hand is that it leaves you in a better position to play another, even if it's in a completely different game.

Finally, a word to people who are considering or who have begun law school in part because they feel burdened by what seem like useless undergraduate degrees. I often hear from prospective or current law students in this situation, and understandably that situation makes such people especially vulnerable to the sunk cost fallacy. They wonder what they're supposed to do with an expensive education that has left them unable to get a decent job, and they tend to feel they have nothing to lose by making another big money bet, even if it's a bad one. Again, this is an understandable thought process, but a very dangerous one. If you find yourself in this position, whatever you do don't get a second, far more expensive and equally useless degree that will, perversely enough, quite possibly make it even harder to get a decent job.

Don't throw good money after bad; don't double down on bad bets; and don't be afraid to fold a losing hand.

What All This Means For You

Most people going to law school today would be better off doing something else. To maximize your chances of being in the minority of law students for who law school will end up being a good decision, it's crucial to be hard-headed about whether trying to become a lawyer really does make sense for you, given the likely costs and benefits.

In this regard, it's especially important to avoid the sunk cost fallacy, and to be willing to walk away from law school not only before you apply or enroll, but even – and indeed especially – afterwards.

15

BEYOND ECONOMIC RISK: DEPRESSION, SUBSTANCE ABUSE AND SUICIDE

This book has focused on the extent to which going to law school has been transformed over the past couple of decades into a high-risk and increasingly unjustifiable economic gamble. But there are other risks associated with law school and the legal profession besides purely monetary ones.

A rich literature has developed on the risks law students and lawyers face from depression, substance abuse, and suicide. It makes for harrowing reading. Consider:

(1) Law students are no more prone to depression than anyone else before starting law school. Yet in the course of law school they develop both clinical and sub-clinical depression at extraordinarily high rates, so that by the time they are 3Ls they are roughly ten times more likely to be suffering from these conditions than they were prior to entering law school.

(2) Rates of depression among practicing attorneys are also very high. For instance, a 1990 Johns Hopkins study looked at depression in 104 occupational groups. Lawyers ranked first.

(3) These findings are remarkably consistent across studies, and have remained so for several decades.

(4) Although there is as of yet little work on what effect recent changes in the legal profession are having on these outcomes, the primary environmental cause of depression appears to be stress, which suggests an already serious problem is likely to be getting worse.

Why are law students and lawyers so prone to develop depression? The literature suggests numerous causes, most of which have something to do with the effects of an intensely hierarchical, competitive, emotionally cold, and high-stress environment, in which people are socialized to obsess on external status markers and to minimize or ignore things such as learning for its own sake, doing intrinsically valuable work, and maintaining healthy personal relationships.

Consider what a typical prospective law student is encouraged to define as success:

(1) Getting into a top law school.
(2) Getting top grades.
(3) Getting a job at a top firm.

There are two problems with these goals. First, the vast majority of law students will fail to achieve them, and will as a result be saddled with enormous educational debts and bad job prospects: an inherently depressing combination. Second, and most interestingly, the academic literature suggests that the few winners in this game appear to be just as prone to depression as the losers. Hierarchical and economic success in law has little correlation with increased happiness. In short, lawyers in Big Law are just as miserable as those outside it, although for somewhat different reasons.

The other consistent finding in this literature is that the one subgroup of lawyers who seem to do significantly better than average in regard to these issues are so-called "cause" lawyers: people who do the work they've taken on primarily for reasons other than money and status. Naturally this finding leads law professors to implore their students to turn their backs on worldly things. What we tend to ignore is that both the increasing cost of legal education and the changing economics of legal practice itself make it very difficult for the vast majority of our students to follow this advice – public service jobs are becoming even harder to acquire than positions with big firms, and of course they pay salaries which make it all but impossible for law students with six-figure educational debt loads to pay back their loans.

Another striking thing about this literature is the legal academy's reaction to it. That reaction tends to be one of, in the words of Lawrence Krieger, one of "individual and institutional avoidance." Krieger is, as the subtitle of one of the articles he's published on this topic affirms, dedicated to breaking the silence about the relationship between legal education, the practice of law, and depression. If all this sounds familiar, so will the reactions Krieger has encountered from other legal academics, which include: it's just as bad in other professional education programs; people come to us that way; it's always been like this; it's the nature of the business; it's not as bad as you say; this requires further study before we do anything; I'm not trained to deal with this; it's somebody else's responsibility; and shut up already.

Depression is not the only occupational hazard that appears among lawyers at much higher rates than in both the general population and among other professionals. Rates of substance abuse, and in particular alcoholism, are strikingly high: several studies have found that 15% to 24% of attorneys are alcoholics (compared to seven percent of the general population), while a recent survey found that fully one third of California lawyers under disciplinary supervision by the state bar were being monitored for substance abuse.

Stress, substance abuse, and depression can form a mutually reinforcing triad with sometimes deadly result: studies of suicide among lawyers find rates that are two to six times higher than that found among people of the same age and gender in the population as a whole. And while there are no general statistics on suicide among law students, the extraordinarily high rates of depression among law students (20% to 40% of law students suffer clinical depression during law school) suggest that they too are at greatly elevated risk for suicide.

It's a platitude that crisis creates opportunity, but platitudes exist because they embody important truths. The truth is that the employment and debt crisis which has been building for many years now among law graduates is creating an opportunity to re-examine and restructure a profession which in many ways needs to change from the ground up, if it is to stop becoming an increasingly efficient machine for producing human misery on a vast scale.

What All This Means For You

Although it's imperative to carefully calculate the economic risk you will face if you enroll in law school, it's no less important to take into account the emotional and psychological dangers law school and the legal profession present. This is especially true if you've already struggled with depression and/or substance abuse. People who have should be especially cautious about entering a profession that poses special risks for them.

Conclusion

Now What? Notes For A Lost Generation

A prospective law student who I advised as he made his way through the 2012 admissions cycle wrote to me the day after he enrolled – with some misgivings – at a top 20 law school, equipped with a scholarship covering two-thirds of his tuition:

> If students who attend most law schools at sticker appear to be irrational, don't blame the students: blame the institutions who create the conditions – and then benefit from those conditions – that render such a horrible deal an arguably rational choice (i.e. the least-worst choice) for hoards of students. How could such a choice possibly be rational?
>
> Because these people think: debt doesn't matter. There is no penalty for defaulting on the debt, except the relinquishment of the privileges of an advanced financial life. . . Students evaluating the horrible deal in question believe they have no access anyway to those privileges (e.g. a retirement account, a home purchase, a start-up business). For the student in question, all law school has to do is provide *some potential benefit*, and it becomes a rational choice.

There's a lot of force in this line of argument – and that is an indictment of not only law schools, but the entire higher education establishment, and indeed the economic and political conditions of contemporary American life.

The law school trap exists in large part because we in legal academia have allowed ourselves to take advantage of a lost generation, made up of millions of bright, highly educated, ambitious young people, who are finding there seems to be no route for them into the professional class they've always been told they would be able to join if they followed all the rules and did everything right.

They did follow all the rules and did everything right – but in America in the second decade of the 21st century, the rules the baby boomers followed don't work nearly as well any more for their own children. One of those rules was that law school was the safe choice for risk-averse liberal arts graduates looking to obtain respectable upper middle class professional identities – and far too many boomer parents have yet to understand that this rule has not only been repealed, but practically inverted.

With few exceptions, law school is now something that only people who are willing to take on high levels of financial and personal risk should consider. The financial risk is clear: law school has gotten so expensive that even someone like my correspondent, who is attending with the benefit of a $105,000 scholarship, will still graduate with around $120,000 in debt. He is attending a school where currently about a quarter of its graduates are obtaining jobs that justify incurring that level of debt – and that's more than double the number of graduates who will obtain such jobs at the average law school.

In other words he is taking a huge financial gamble (and not just a financial gamble: see Chapter 15), but at least he's doing so with his eyes open. He is very much part of a generation that increasingly finds itself without good life options, and he may very well be making the best of a bad situation. But keep in mind that he's someone who scored in the 98th percentile of the LSAT, and is attending a top 20 law school with the benefit of a six-figure scholarship. That doing so is only arguably his least-worst option is, again, very much an indictment of both law schools in particular, and our current educational and economic system in general.

So where does all this leave the recent or not so recent college graduate, who is looking for a way out of the highly educated underemployment that has overtaken an entire generation of young Americans? What, I have been asked many times in the last few years by people in this position, are we supposed to do?

It's an excellent question, and good answer to it would require knowing much more than I do about the particular life circumstances of those who ask it. So the only answer I can give is a cautionary one: if you're thinking about going to law school, do your best to make sure you're not making a difficult situation worse. If you find you can't get into any of the tiny and shrinking handful (and by handful I mean three to six) of law schools that remain reasonable choices for many people even when paying full tuition, and if you don't have the option of attending any of the other seven to ten truly national law schools at a significantly reduced price, or any of three dozen or so good regional schools for little or nothing more than the opportunity cost, then you should wait.

Do something – anything – other than attend an average law school at the average price. If you insist on doing so you're likely to experience what is now the average result for law graduates, which is something between a serious disappointment and a life-wrecking disaster. In two or three or five years, the law schools will still be here (most of them anyway). Maybe by then law schools will be a lot cheaper, or job prospects for lawyers will stop deteriorating, or both.

But while that may be then, this is now. Don't catch a falling knife.

TL;DR: BAD REASONS FOR GOING TO LAW SCHOOL

There are many bad reasons to go to law school. Here are a few:

(8) **Everybody in my family is a lawyer**

Is everybody in your family also a workaholic with a drinking problem who hates their spouse and never sees their kids? As bad reasons go this is a relatively benign one – maybe somebody close to you can help get you a job – but do you really want to have the same life as that person? And law professors may not know very much about the actual practice of law, but I've been struck over the years by how few of them seem to have any interest in encouraging their children to become lawyers.

(7) **I want to help poor people/save mountaintops from being blown up in West Virginia/stop human right violations in Africa/ make a difference in this world.**

Cynical law students tend to dismiss their classmates' interest in doing anything but trying to make money by pointing out how these noble ideals soon crumble in the face of the realities of On Campus Interviewing. But that's the point: It turns out there's very little money in law for doing anything other than representing the interests of the rich and powerful. That doesn't mean people who claimed to want to do something else were disingenuous – more likely they were merely naïve. If you want to go to law school to help poor people, please keep in mind that in early 21st century America nobody who matters cares about the interests of poor people, so unless you're independently wealthy or extremely lucky you will not be able to help poor people by going to law school.

(6) **I want to be rich**

Going to law school in order to become rich is a bad idea. Very few lawyers end up making big money, even loosely defined. If you're very fortunate you'll make just enough money to feel poor by comparison to the vastly wealthier people you'll be dealing with regularly in your professional life. Plus you'll be making about $17 an hour. Go try to become an investment banker if working insane hours in the pursuit of filthy lucre is your thing.

(5) **Lawyers do all kinds of interesting work**

I once saw a T-shirt emblazoned with this message: "Everything You've Learned From TV Is Wrong." Words of wisdom Lloyd, words of wisdom. Most legal work is boring and stressful. Not surprisingly most lawyers are bored, stressed people. (That is, the ones who actually have jobs. Let's not get ahead of ourselves.)

(4) **None of this is relevant to me, because I'm going to graduate in the top ten percent of my class from an elite law school, work at a big firm for five years while living like a monk to pay off my debts, and then do what I really wanted to do all along**

You get the hell out of here.

(3) **My parents will be disappointed in me if I don't do something respectable instead of pursuing my dream of being a ____**

Semi-employed permanent bankruptcy is in no way respectable, and there's a very real risk that that's where going to law school will leave you. Your parents don't understand this because their knowledge of what being a lawyer entails is based on TV (see (5), *supra*).

If you want to write the Great American Novel you'll probably fail, but it won't be the kind of failure that produces $200,000 in non-discharge-able debt while filling you with self-loathing.

(2) What am I supposed to do with this useless undergraduate degree in English/PoliSci/Sociology/Assyrian Musicology?

It's a fair question. Here's the best answer I've got: *Don't double down on useless degrees.* People who already have educational debt from undergrad and then borrow $250,000 in tuition and living expenses to go to law school are like people in a terrible relationship who decide to have a baby because maybe the kid will bring them closer together.

(1) I don't know what to do with my life

Have you ever said to yourself, "I don't know what to do with my life – so I'm going to spend three years of it going deeply and irrevers-ibly into debt, in a quite possibly futile attempt to enter a profession that I have no actual desire to join?" I bet you haven't, because who would ever say something that idiotic? Every year, however, thou-sands of people are perfectly capable of *doing* something that idiotic. If they weren't, half the law schools in the country would be out of business tomorrow.

Made in the USA
San Bernardino, CA
19 June 2017